Fabulous!

Fabulous! Food that Makes You Feel Good
Volume 1: Desserts

ISBN: 978-0-9818488-9-1
Printed in the United States of America
©2009, 2010 by Laura Kurella
All rights reserved

Second Edition: March 2010

Photography & Interior Design by Laura Kurella
Cover design by Isaac Publishing, Inc.

Library of Congress Cataloging-in-Publication Data

IPI
Isaac Publishing, Inc.
P.O. 342
Three Rivers, MI 49093
www.isaacpublishing.com

No part of this book may be reproduced or transmitted in any form or by any means, electronic or mechanical—including photocopying, recording, or by any information storage and retrieval system—without permission in writing from the publisher, except as provided by United States of America copyright law.

Please direct your inquiries to admin@isaacpublishing.com

Volume I: Desserts

Food that makes you feel good

By Laura Kurella

Food That Makes You Feel Good!

Introduction

This book would not have been possible had it not been for the tremendous support it received from 3 remarkable women: Kathi Livermore, Anne Sutton and Rebecca Reeg.

These ladies are truly my, "Angels in the Outfield." They'd have to be to take on a cookbook written by a dyslexic south paw who holed up 8 years worth of typos, errors and inconsistencies. I think God sent them Himself because He knew I needed all the patience, understanding and eagle eyes I could get. Thank you ladies and God bless you!

I'd also like to thank my family and friends, most especially my daughter Elyse, for being so patient and understanding with me over the tremendous amount of time I pour into my work. Your understanding means the world to me. Thank you, sweetie!

And finally, I'd like to thank you for opening this book. It means that you are looking to feel better with food that makes you feel good.

As you flip through this book you will notice that there is no regime or strict diets or food plans involved – nope! In fact, I've written it in a chocolate font so it is as delicious and fun to read as the recipes are to eat!

Food should be fun and pleasurable - as God intended, and my philosophy on achieving better health is just that - listen to the one who knows best about our body's needs – God.

If we eat more of what comes straight from the earth - God's hand - we cannot go wrong, even with desserts!

By enjoying a variety of food, especially all the natural delights that come directly from the earth, you will begin to look and feel better, too.

Variety is indeed, the spice of life and it is my greatest hope that this first recipe volume, "Desserts," will aid you in adding more earthly varieties into your diet and thusly, make a positive difference in how you look and how you feel...one recipe at a time.

Enjoy!

Laura

Please Note: The nutritional information provided with the recipes contained herein are approximations and should be considered as a guide only, not actual figures.

Food That Makes You Feel Good!

Food That Makes You Feel Good!

Bundt cake revival!

The popularity of a bundt cake may have waned, but the thought of sinking your fork into a tall slice of a moist and luscious Choc-choc-chocolate Bundt Cake, dripping in an amazing chocolate glaze is enough to cause a bundt cake revival!

Does anyone remember when bundt cakes first came out? Well I do and boy was I impressed at how beautiful they looked and tasted.

When I found out all that it took was a pan, I immediately ran out and bought the cheapest one I could find then promptly planned a dinner party around it.

But, as all good plans can go awry, I found out quickly that bundts weren't that easy, especially when it came time to get mine out of its cheap pan.

That cake refused to let go of the pan, and I do mean REFUSED! I fought with it and fought with it and even went so far as to throw the darn thing back in the oven then yank it out and plunge the pan into an ice bath, thinking it would cause the cake to pull away from the pan like a cooked egg pulls away from its shell - NOT! Instead, the pan just hissed at me and in an odd tone that almost sounded like it was laughing. That really ticked me off!

Here I was, in the middle of my now destroyed kitchen with my dessert stuck in its pan and guests arriving in less than 2 hours!

I became desperate, and desperate times call for desperate actions so without a second thought I reached for a knife and used it to hastily pry that poor cake out of its metal prison.

Needless to say, this action left my cake appearing to be anything but desirable.
No longer did I have a beautiful bundt cake before me. Rather, it resembled something brown that might have been thrown off the top of 4 story building. Dessert suicide, indeed!

I did save it - in a sense, by scooping up the crumbly cake and sprinkling it between scoops of ice cream layered in tall parfait glasses, so all was not lost. Well, everything but the pan, that is. I threw that one away!

I did learn some valuable lessons from that bundt cake: Don't count your chickens before they're hatched, and never buy a cheap pan or you will live to regret it!

Since that day, I also made it a point to learn what to do with a stuck cake so I never find myself in that situation again without a plan in hand. Here are two top tips:
1. Try wrapping cake pan bottom and sides in a towel soaked in very hot water.
2. Try freezing cake in the pan. It should come out once frozen.

Bundt cakes are beautiful and very delicious. Plus, they make a great gift and require little effort to look beautiful - if you treat that pan right!

Lemon-licious Bundt Cake

CAKE
1 18 ounce box lemon cake mix
1 3 ounce box instant lemon pudding mix
4 extra large eggs
1 cup sour cream
2 teaspoons lemon extract, optional
juice of 1 lemon
finely grated rind of 1 lemon
1/2 cup vegetable oil

GLAZE
1 1/2 cups powdered sugar
3 tablespoons half & half or whole milk
1/4 teaspoon pure vanilla extract

CAKE: Preheat oven to 325 degrees. Butter a 12 inch bundt pan. In a mixer bowl, combine cake mix, pudding mix, eggs, sour cream, lemon extract, juice and rind and the oil. Bake as directed on cake box or until a toothpick inserted in center comes out clean.
GLAZE: Combine powdered sugar, half and half or milk and vanilla extract then pour over cooled cake.

Approximate servings per recipe: 16.
Per serving: Calories 271; Fat 15g; Sodium 308 mg; Carbohydrates 31g; Fiber 0.4g; Sugar 14g; Protein 4.

Rum-dilly Bundt Cake

CAKE
1 cup chopped pecans or walnuts
1 package yellow cake mix
1 package vanilla instant pudding mix
4 large eggs
1/2 cup cold water
1/2 cup vegetable oil
1/2 cup amber rum

GLAZE
1/2 cup butter
1/4 cup water
1 cup granulated sugar
1/2 cup amber rum

CAKE: Preheat oven to 325 degrees. Sprinkle nuts over bottom of greased 10 inch tube pan or 12 cup bundt pan. Stir together cake mix, pudding mix, eggs, water, oil and rum. Pour batter over nuts. Bake for 1 hour. Cool 10 minutes in pan. Invert onto serving plate and prick top.
GLAZE: Melt butter in saucepan. Stir in water and sugar. Boil 5 minutes, stirring constantly. Remove from heat. Stir in rum. Brush glaze evenly over top and sides of cake. Allow cake to absorb glaze.

Approximate servings per recipe: 20.
Per serving: Calories 309; Fat 18g; Sodium 288 mg; Carbohydrates 35g; Fiber 1g; Sugar 25g; Protein 3g.

Food That Makes You Feel Good!

Banana-rama Bundt Cake

CAKE
1 1/2 cups mashed ripe bananas
2 teaspoons freshly squeezed lemon juice
3 cups all purpose flour
1 1/2 teaspoons baking soda
1/4 teaspoon salt
3/4 cup butter, softened
2 1/8 cups granulated sugar
3 large eggs
2 teaspoons pure vanilla extract
1 1/2 cups well shaken buttermilk

FROSTING
1/2 cup butter, softened
1 eight ounce package cream cheese, softened
1 teaspoon pure vanilla extract
3 1/2 cups powdered sugar

CAKE: Preheat oven to 300 degrees. Grease and flour a 10 inch bundt pan. In a small bowl, mix mashed banana with the lemon juice and set aside. In a medium bowl, mix flour, baking soda and salt and set aside. In a large bowl, cream butter and sugar until light and fluffy. Beat in eggs, one at a time, then stir in vanilla. Beat in the flour mixture alternately with the buttermilk. Stir in banana mixture. Pour batter into prepared pan and bake for one hour or until toothpick inserted in center comes out clean. Important: Remove from oven and place directly into the freezer for 45 minutes. This will make the cake very moist.
FROSTING: In a mixing bowl, cream butter and cream cheese until smooth.
Beat in vanilla. Add powdered sugar and beat on low speed until combined, then on high speed until frosting is smooth. Spread on cooled cake.

Approximate servings per recipe: 16. Per serving: Calories 504; Fat 20g; Sodium 336 mg; Carbohydrates 75g; Fiber 1g; Sugar 55g; Protein 6g.

Great Cakes Alive!

Food That Makes You Feel Good!

Good things take time, but with the world spinning faster than ever, time has become a commodity, leaving things like cake baking behind.

Obviously, there is a convenience to commercial baked goods. They do make it very easy for us to "grab and go," but that doesn't mean we shouldn't on occasion take the time to whip up something wonderful in our own kitchen.

Home baking is not only a rewarding and delicious way to spend some time, but it also - more often than not - creates confections that are lower in calories and fat than their commercial counterparts. Now that's something to chew on!

We are blessed to live in a day and age where the art of home cake baking has become somewhat of a science and we can thank Henry Baker for providing one of tastiest cake chemistry lessons ever.

In 1927, Henry Baker was an insurance salesman and an avid baker who struck upon a way to make his chiffon cake light and fluffy. He simply used salad oil instead of butter or lard in his batter, which created a sponge-like texture that was very moist and very pleasing. So pleasing, in fact, that Henry was able to sell his special cakes to various restaurants.

In 1948, he sold his recipe to General Mills who began touting it on their Betty Crocker radio show as "the cake discovery of the century" and then started inserting his recipe in specially marked bags of Gold Metal flour.

In roughly one year, Betty Crocker came out with a line of boxed cake mixes featuring Henry's golden secret - a move that changed home cake baking forever!

Caramel Apple Cake

This cake is very easy to make and very delightful to eat, especially in autumn.

CAKE
1 2 layer size package yellow cake mix
1 4 serving size package French vanilla instant pudding & pie filling
1 cup water
4 large eggs
1/3 cup canola oil
3 Granny Smith apples, peeled, cored and chopped

GLAZE
20 caramels, unwrapped
1/4 cup milk

CAKE: Preheat oven to 350 degrees. Grease and flour a 10 inch tube pan. With a mixer, in a large bowl, combine cake mix, pudding mix, water, eggs and oil on low speed until blended. Beat on high speed 2 minutes then gently stir in apples. Pour into prepared pan. Bake 50 minutes to 1 hour or until toothpick inserted in center comes out clean. Cool 20 minutes then remove from pan and cool completely on wire rack.

GLAZE: In a glass 2 cup liquid measure, combine caramels and milk. Microwave on high for 1 1/2 minutes, stirring every 30 seconds, until melted and blended. Cool until slightly thickened then drizzle over cake.

Approximate servings per recipe: 16.
Per serving: Calories 110; Fat 6g;
Carbohydrates 4g; Fiber 0.62g; Protein 2g.

Great Cakes Alive!

The popularity of a bundt cake may have waned, but the thought of sinking a fork into a tall slice of moist and luscious Choc-choc-chocolate Bundt Cake, dripping in a chocolate glaze is enough to cause a bundt cake revival!

Food That Makes You Feel Good!

Choc-choc-chocolate Bundt Cake

CAKE
1 18 1/4 ounce package devil's food cake mix
4 ounces instant chocolate pudding mix
2 cups semisweet chocolate chips
1 3/4 cups water
2 large eggs, beaten
1 teaspoon pure vanilla extract

GLAZE
3 tablespoons cocoa powder
2 tablespoons butter, melted
1 cup powdered sugar
2 to 3 tablespoons hot water

CAKE: Preheat oven to 325 degrees. Grease and flour a 10 inch bundt pan. In large mixing bowl, combine cake mix, pudding mix and chocolate chips. In another bowl, combine water, eggs and vanilla, mixing well. Add egg mixture to dry mixture and mix with spoon until blended. Pour into prepared pan and bake for 50 minutes or until cake tests done when wooden pick inserted in center comes out clean. Cool 15 to 20 minutes before removing cake from pan.

GLAZE: In a small bowl, combine cocoa powder melted butter, powdered sugar and 2 to 3 tablespoons hot water, stirring with a spoon until smooth.
When cake is completely cool, drizzle with chocolate glaze.

Approximate servings per recipe: 16. Per serving: Calories 319; Fat 14g; Sodium 390 mg; Carbohydrates 51g; Fiber 3g; Sugar 35g; Protein 4g.

Great Cakes Alive!

There is a secret place in everybody's heart that longs for those simple, old fashioned favorites, like a smooth and buttery slice of a moist and delicious pound cake.

Food That Makes You Feel Good!

On Golden Pound

There is just something about a pound cake that makes it delightfully different.

It tastes great eaten alone, drizzled with glaze, slathered with butter or as the base of another dessert, like strawberries and cream.

Some even grill it. Yes, by beating an egg with two tablespoons of milk and two more of Grand Marnier, then dipping some cake slices into it, as you would French Toast, you can pop them on the grill and, after browning on both sides, create an even more decadent dessert - oh my!

Pound cake came from the English several centuries ago and its name comes from the fact that the cake originally contained one pound of each ingredient: butter, sugar, eggs and flour.

This easy, off-the top-of-your-head kind of recipe was very popular back in the days when many people could not read.

In the original recipe, no leavening agents were used. The cake relied solely on the air whipped into the batter, which caused those early cakes to be far denser than they are today.

By the mid 1800's, pound cake recipes began to deviate slightly from the original formula in order to make a lighter cake.

Some recipes tried using liquids, such as alcohol or rose water, but it wasn't until the 20th century that artificial leavening agents, baking powder and/or baking soda, were finally added.

While today's pound cake does use different proportions, most are still made with the same key ingredients.

Butter is very important in this recipe and only the finest should be used. It serves to add moistness and richness not found in any other cake and actually lightens the cake by trapping air bubbles during mixing process.

Bringing the dairy products to room temperature will help ensure good aeration. However, if the butter isn't beaten long enough, you could still end up with a dense cake. Adding a little baking powder will ensure your cake will rise either way.

Butter also makes the cake more tender. It does so by coating the flour proteins so that gluten, a substance that makes cake tough, cannot form.

To improve your odds at making a really soft, tender cake try using a low protein cake flour instead of an all purpose flour.

To guarantee a moist cake try glazing it. Poking holes in the cake while it's still hot will help the cake absorb the glaze and don't be afraid to go deep because the deeper you go, the better the cake will taste so, dig in!

Great Cakes Alive!

Buttery Buttermilk Pound Cake
1 cup butter, softened
2 cups granulated sugar
4 large eggs, room temperature
3 cups cake flour
1/2 teaspoon baking soda
1/4 teaspoon salt
1 cup well shaken buttermilk
1 teaspoon pure vanilla extract
1 teaspoon pure lemon extract

Preheat oven to 325 degrees. Cream butter, gradually add sugar, beating at medium speed of an electric mixer until well blended. Add eggs, one at a time, beating after each addition. Combine flour, soda, and salt then add to creamed mixture alternately with buttermilk, beginning and ending with flour mixture. Stir in extracts then pour into greased and floured 10 inch tube pan. Bake at 325 degrees for 1 hour or until a toothpick inserted in the center comes out clean.

Approximate servings per recipe: 24. Per serving: Calories 206; Fat 7g; Carbohydrates 29g: Fiber 0.4g; Sugar 17g; Protein 3g.

Tastes Like Store Bought Pound Cake
1/2 pound butter, softened
2 cups powdered sugar
3 large eggs, room temperature
1 2/3 cups cake flour
1 tablespoon pure vanilla extract

Preheat the oven to 325 degrees. Spray an 8 1/2 inch glass loaf pan with cooking spray. Cream the butter with the powdered sugar on high speed of mixer for 5 minutes. Add 1 egg and then a little flour, beating 2 minutes. Add second egg and half of remaining flour and beat 2 minutes. Add third egg, the rest of the flour and the vanilla, beating 2 more minutes. Spread batter evenly in prepared loaf pan. Bake 65 minutes or until tester inserted into the center comes out clean. Cool in the baking pan on a wire rack for 30 minutes before removing from pan.

Servings per recipe: 10. Per serving: Calories 354; Fat 20g; Carbohydrates 40g: Fiber 1g; Sugar 23g; Protein 4g.

Food That Makes You Feel Good!

Chocolate Pound Cake
3 1/2 cups flour
1 cup unsweetened cocoa powder
2 teaspoons ground cinnamon
2 teaspoons baking powder
1/2 teaspoon salt
1 pound unsalted butter, at room temp
2 cups light brown sugar
1 cup sugar
6 eggs, at room temp
1/2 cup whole milk, at room temp
1/2 cup strong coffee, at room temp
1 teaspoon vanilla

Preheat oven to 350 degrees. Generously grease and flour 2 loaf pans or 1 bundt pan. Sift the flour, cocoa powder, cinnamon, baking powder and salt into a bowl. Place the butter and sugars in mixer bowl and beat until smooth and creamy. Add eggs, one at a time, beating well. Add half the flour mixture and beat well, then add the milk, coffee and vanilla.
Add remaining flour mixture. Beat well then pour batter into prepared pan(s). Bake until cake pulls away from the sides and tester comes out NOT QUITE clean, approx. 50-55 minutes for bundt pan, 45 minutes for 9x5, and 40 minutes for 8x4's. Cool for 20 minutes in pan, then invert on rack. Cool to room temperature.

Approximate servings per recipe: 24.
Per serving: Calories 307; Fat 16g; Sodium 125mg; Carbohydrates 35g; Fiber 0.5g; Sugar 25g; Protein 4g.

Easy Cheesy Pound Cake
1 1/2 cups butter
8 ounces cream cheese, softened
3 cups sugar
6 eggs
3 cups flour
1 teaspoon vanilla

GARNISH (optional)
1/2 cup melted caramel

Preheat oven to 325 degrees.
Cream butter, cream cheese and sugar together. Add eggs one at a time then add vanilla then flour, slowly. Pour into a lightly greased bundt or tube pan. Bake for 1-1/2 hours.
GARNISH: Drizzle with 1/2 cup melted caramel.

Approximate servings per recipe: 24.
Per serving: Calories 307; Fat 16g; Sodium 125mg; Carbohydrates 35g; Fiber 0.5g; Sugar 25g; Protein 4g.

Great Cakes Alive!

Food That Makes You Feel Good!

Luscious 'n' Lemony Pound Cake

3 cups cake flour
1 teaspoon baking powder
1 teaspoon fine sea salt
4 large eggs, beaten, at room temperature
1 cup half and half
1/2 teaspoon pure lemon extract
1/2 cup butter, softened
4 ounces cream cheese, softened
2 cups granulated sugar
1 tablespoon finely grated lemon rind
2 tablespoons poppy seeds (optional)

GLAZE
3/4 cup freshly squeezed lemon juice, strained
3/4 cup granulated sugar
1 1/2 cups powdered sugar
3 tablespoons half and half
1/4 teaspoon pure vanilla extract

FROSTING
1 1/2 cups powdered sugar
3 tablespoons half and half or whole milk
1/4 teaspoon pure vanilla extract

Preheat oven to 325 degrees. Butter a 12 inch bundt pan. Into a medium bowl, sift flour, baking powder and salt. In a large measuring cup whisk together the beaten eggs, the 1 cup half and half and the lemon extract. In a larger mixer bowl, blend butter and cream cheese, beating well, and then add the sugar, and lemon rind. Beat until nice and fluffy, about 8 minutes. With mixer running on lowest speed, alternately add flour mixture and egg mixture to butter, blending well after each addition. Fold in poppy seeds then pour batter into prepared pan. Bake for about 1 hour, or until a toothpick inserted in the center comes out clean.
GLAZE: While cake is baking, simmer lemon juice and sugar in a small saucepan until sugar dissolves. While cake is still hot, poke dozens of holes deep into the cake with a thin bamboo skewer or large toothpick. Drizzle half of the glaze over the cake. Let cake cool for 20 minutes then invert onto a serving platter and brush remaining glaze over top of cake. Let cool completely.
FROSTING: Combine powdered sugar, half and half or milk and vanilla extract then pour over cooled cake.

Approximate servings per recipe: 24. Per serving: Calories 293; Fat 9g; Carbohydrates 50g; Fiber 0.5g; Sugar 36g; Protein 3g.

Great Cakes Alive!

Food That Makes You Feel Good!

Better cake baking made easy!

All cooks have their own way of doings things, which is why one recipe will taste completely different in someone else's hands.

Baking demands accuracy, which is why it's important to follow a baking recipe to the letter, and there are some very good reasons why.

Take butter. When a recipe calls for it to be softened or at room temperature it's because the recipe depends upon the butter's viscosity to trap tiny little air bubbles, thus giving your cake or muffin a more delicate texture once baked.

The physical properties of butter are changed when melted and prevent butter from being gathered as well as mixing properly with the flour.

If butter is softened too much, to the point where fingers go all the way through the stick when touched, or melted, it will not incorporate air or get fluffy when mixed (creamed). The water or liquid part of the butter will also be released and will make dough tough.

To soften butter quickly, cut it into chunks and allow it to soften at room temperature about 15 minutes. If time is limited, place an unwrapped stick of cold butter between sheets of waxed paper and hit it with a rolling pin on each side to smash it into a thin layer to warm it quicker.

The Land O'Lakes Test Kitchens recommend that you do not soften butter in the microwave for use in baking.

Then there are the eggs. An egg's cooking properties are so varied that they have been called "the cement that holds the castle of cuisine together," so when a recipe calls for eggs in a specific way, please take notice.

Size does matter! Grades of eggs are defined by the USDA and though any size egg may be used for frying, scrambling, cooking in the shell or poaching, most recipes for baking have been developed on the basis of a large egg unless otherwise specified. If not specified, it's best to use a large anyway.

Temperature also matters, especially in cakes. If cold eggs are introduced to a room temperature butter and sugar mixture, the emulsion can break and the batter will lose air cells. The result can be a cake or muffin that is grainy or flat in texture, dry and flavorless, look uneven and may even sink.

To bring an egg up to room temperature quickly, remove eggs from the refrigerator about 20 to 30 minutes before you use them or put them in a bowl of warm water while you assemble other ingredients. Be sure to dry them with a towel before cracking.

By following instructions as written we can all have a winning cake recipe every time!

Great Cakes Alive!

Food That Makes You Feel Good!

Chocolate Potato Cake
CAKE
1 large Idaho potato, peeled, cooked and mashed
1 cup granulated sugar
1 cup brown sugar
2 teaspoons Irish cream liqueur
1 cup liquid egg substitute
3/4 cup unsweetened cocoa powder
1 cup all purpose flour
1 teaspoon baking powder

FROSTING
4 ounces unsweetened dark chocolate
4 ounces skim milk
4 cups powdered sugar
3 tablespoons Irish cream liqueur

CAKE: Preheat oven to 375 degrees. With cooking spray, lightly coat a 9x13 inch glass or metal baking pan. In an electric mixer bowl, combine mashed potato, granulated sugar, brown sugar, Irish cream and egg substitute. Mix until blended, then stir in cocoa, flour and baking powder. Mix until all ingredients are blended. Pour into prepared pan and bake 25 minutes or until top is springy. Cool cake completely before frosting cake.
FROSTING: In a 4 cup glass liquid measure, melt chocolate in microwave, stirring at 15 second intervals, pour into a medium bowl. Stir in milk and Irish cream then add sugar by the cupful. Add more milk if a thinner consistency is desired. Pour over cooled cake.
Note: Can also be made using milk chocolate or light cocoa.
Simply adjust milk for desired consistency.

Approximate servings per recipe: 24. Per serving: Calories 103; Fat 0.44g; Carbohydrates 23g; Fiber 1g; Protein 2g.

Great Cakes Alive!

Food That Makes You Feel Good!

Green Apple Cake

4 large eggs
1/2 cup granulated sugar
1/2 cup apple juice concentrate
1/4 cup skim milk
4 tablespoons butter, melted
2 teaspoons pure vanilla extract
2 cups self rising flour
3 tablespoons cornstarch
2 large green apples, peeled, cored and minced
2 teaspoons cinnamon
Green Food Coloring (optional)

Preheat the oven to 400 degrees. Spray two 8 inch round cake pans with cooking spray. With an electric mixer, beat eggs and sugar until light and fluffy. Stir in juice, milk, butter and vanilla then add 5 drops of green food coloring, if using. In a small bowl, combine flour and cornstarch then fold into cake batter. Sprinkle apples with cinnamon then fold into batter. Pour batter into prepared cake pans and bake for 30 minutes or until toothpick inserted in center comes out clean.
Cool and frost with Better Than Buttercream Frosting, if desired.

Approximate servings per recipe: 8. Per serving: Calories 278; Fat 3g; Carbohydrates 47g; Fiber 1g; Protein 7g.

Better Than Buttercream Frosting

8 ounces Neufchatel cheese, softened
1/4 cup butter, softened
3 cups powdered sugar
1 teaspoon pure vanilla extract

In a large mixing bowl, beat cream cheese and butter at high speed until fluffy, about 1 minute. Beat in powdered sugar, 1 cup at a time, then continue beating until smooth. Beat in vanilla. Chill bowl of frosting in refrigerator, stirring often, until good spreading consistency. Makes about 2 2/3 cups.

Approximate servings per recipe: 24. Calories 40; Fat 2g; Sodium 15mg; Carbohydrate 5g; Fiber 0g; Sugars 6g; Protein 0.5g.

Great Cakes Alive!

The boxed cake mix was instantly adored and called the best cake recipe to come along in over 100 years, resulting in the nationwide cake baking craze of the 1950's.

Cake baking contests popped up all over and garden themed cakes became the rage.

Pink Azalea cakes were popular, as was the Brown Eyed Susan cake, which perfectly pairs the flavors of chocolate and orange.

To honor the ladies who created all those trendy, tantalizing treats, here are some of the more popular Garden Cake recipes that helped the cake kingdom bloom!

Food That Makes You Feel Good!

Brown Eyed Susan Cake
1 yellow cake mix, batter prepared
5 ounces unsweetened chocolate, melted
2 teaspoons grated orange rind
4 cups vanilla butter cream frosting
1 tablespoon orange juice
2 drops yellow food coloring
semisweet chocolate chips
dried pineapple slices
Best Buttercream Frosting

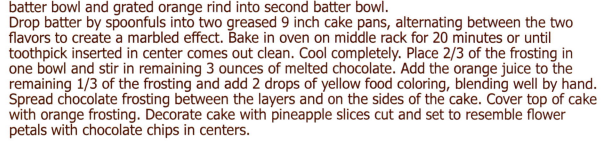

Preheat oven to 350 degrees. Divide batter between two bowls. Stir 2 ounces of melted chocolate into one batter bowl and grated orange rind into second batter bowl.
Drop batter by spoonfuls into two greased 9 inch cake pans, alternating between the two flavors to create a marbled effect. Bake in oven on middle rack for 20 minutes or until toothpick inserted in center comes out clean. Cool completely. Place 2/3 of the frosting in one bowl and stir in remaining 3 ounces of melted chocolate. Add the orange juice to the remaining 1/3 of the frosting and add 2 drops of yellow food coloring, blending well by hand. Spread chocolate frosting between the layers and on the sides of the cake. Cover top of cake with orange frosting. Decorate cake with pineapple slices cut and set to resemble flower petals with chocolate chips in centers.

Approximate servings per recipe: 12. Per serving: Calories 260; Fat 9g; Carbohydrates 30g; Fiber 1g; Protein 3g.

Best Buttercream Frosting
1/3 cup vegetable shortening
1/3 cup butter, softened
5 tablespoons half and half
1/8 teaspoon salt
2 teaspoons vanilla
3 1/2 cups powdered sugar
In a large bowl of an electric mixer, at medium speed beat together shortening, butter, half and half, salt and vanilla until smooth (about 3 minutes). Add powdered sugar, 1/2 cup at a time, beating very well until smooth and fluffy. Add more sugar or half and half to achieve desired consistency.

Approximate servings per recipe: 12. Per serving: Calories 123; Fat 6g; Sodium 25mg; Carbohydrate 17g; Fiber 0g; Sugars 17g; Protein 0.25g.

Great Cakes Alive!

The Pink Azalea Cake

1 cup all purpose flour
2 teaspoons baking powder
1 teaspoon baking soda
1/4 teaspoon salt
1 1/2 cups granulated sugar, divided use
4 large eggs, separated
1/2 cup vegetable oil
1/3 cup water
2 teaspoons pure vanilla extract
2 large egg whites
2 drops red food coloring
1 recipe Seven Minute Frosting
2 drops red food coloring
1/4 cup chopped Maraschino cherries
1/4 cup chopped walnuts

Position rack in center of oven and preheat to 350 degrees. Grease and flour two 9 inch round cake pans. Sift together flour, baking powder, baking soda, salt and 1 cup of sugar. Set aside. In a large bowl of an electric mixer, beat egg yolks at high speed. Turn speed to low and pour in oil, water and vanilla. Gradually add the sifted ingredients and when almost incorporated, turn speed to medium and beat until well combined. Remove bowl from machine. With another large mixer bowl, using whisk attachment, whip the six egg whites until soft peaks form, starting on medium speed and raising speed as peaks begin to form. Gradually pour in the remaining 1/2 cup sugar and whip until whites are shiny and firm but not stiff. With a rubber spatula, fold 1/4 of the whites into the cake mixture, then scrape the cake mixture back into the whites, quickly folding until completely incorporated. Pour one quarter of the batter into each of the two pans. Tint remaining half of the batter pink with red food coloring. Pour an equal amount into center of the batter in both pans. Take a toothpick and zigzag through the pans to make pink swirl in the batter. Bake until a tester inserted into the center of the cakes comes out clean, about 15 minutes. Cool on a rack.
FROSTING: In a medium bowl, tint half of the Seven Minute frosting pink with red food coloring. Stir the cherries and nuts into the remaining frosting. Spread cherry and nut frosting between layers and frost cake with pink frosting.

Approximate servings per recipe: 12. Per serving: Calories 254; Fat 10g; Carbohydrates 36g; Fiber 2g; Protein 4g.

Seven Minute Frosting

2 large egg whites
1 1/2 cups granulated sugar
1/3 cup cold water
1 1/2 teaspoons light corn syrup
1 teaspoon pure vanilla extract

In the top pot of a double boiler, combine egg whites, sugar, water and syrup. Using a hand held electric mixer, beat ingredients until well mixed. Place pot over rapidly boiling water in bottom pot and, using electric mixer, beat constantly while it cooks for 7 minutes or until it will stand in peaks when beater is raised. Remove from heat. Beat in vanilla. Frosting will fill and frost a 2 layer cake, 8 or 9 inches.

Approximate servings per recipe: 12.
Per serving: Calories: 103; Fat 0g;
Carbohydrates: 26g; Protein: 0.6g.

Food That Makes You Feel Good!

German Chocolate Cake

CAKE
2 cups cake flour
1 teaspoon baking soda
1/4 teaspoon salt
1 cup butter, softened
2 cups sugar
4 eggs, separated
4 ounces sweet dark chocolate, melted
1 teaspoon vanilla extract
1 cup buttermilk

FROSTING
1 (12 ounce) can evaporated milk
1 1/2 cups sugar
3/4 cup butter
4 egg yolks, slightly beaten
2 teaspoons vanilla extract
7 ounces shredded coconut
1 1/2 cups chopped pecans

Preheat oven to 350 degrees. Grease and flour the bottoms of 3 (9") round cake pans, and line with wax paper. In a bowl, sift together flour, baking soda and salt; set aside. In the bowl of an electric mixer, cream butter and sugar on medium speed until light and fluffy, about 5 minutes. Add egg yolks, 1 at a time, beating well after each addition. Stir in melted chocolate and vanilla. Add flour mixture alternately with buttermilk, beating well after each addition. In a separate bowl, beat egg whites with electric mixer on high speed until stiff peaks form. Fold into your batter. Pour evenly into prepared pans. Bake for 30 minutes or until toothpick inserted in centers comes out clean. Immediately run spatula between cakes and sides of pans. Cool 15 minutes then remove from pans. Remove wax paper and cool completely on wire racks.
FROSTING: In a large saucepan over medium high heat, combine milk, sugar, butter, egg yolks and vanilla, stirring constantly, cook for 12 minutes or until thickened and golden brown. Remove from heat. Stir in coconut and pecans. Cool to room temperature and of spreading consistency. Spread between each layer then over top and sides of cake.

Approximate servings per recipe: 24. Per serving: Calories 422; Fat 27g; Sodium 234mg; Carbohydrate 45g; Fiber 2g; Sugars 33g; Protein 6g.

Great Cakes Alive!

Food That Makes You Feel Good!

Lemon Garden Cake

1/2 pound unsalted butter, room temperature
2 cups granulated sugar
4 large eggs, room temperature
1/3 cup grated lemon zest
3 cups flour
1/2 teaspoon baking powder
1/2 teaspoon baking soda
1/2 teaspoon fine sea salt
1/4 cup fresh lemon juice
3/4 cup buttermilk, room temperature
1 teaspoon vanilla extract
1 Buttercream Frosting recipe (on page 29)

Preheat oven to 350 degrees. Grease and flour 2 9 inch round cake pans, lining the bottom with parchment paper, if desired. In the bowl of an electric mixer, cream butter and 2 cups granulated sugar until light and fluffy, approximately 5 minutes. Then with mixer on medium speed, add eggs, 1 at a time, and lemon zest. In a separate bowl, sift together flour, baking powder, baking soda and salt. In another bowl, combine lemon juice, buttermilk and vanilla. Alternately add flour and buttermilk mixtures to batter. Divide batter evenly between pans, smoothing the tops. Bake 45 minutes to 1 hour or until tester comes out clean. When cakes are done, cool 10 minutes before removing from pans. Allow cakes to cool completely before frosting.

FROSTING: Decorate cake with buttercream frosting, if desired, by tinting 3/4 of the frosting green and 1/4 of the frosting yellow. Frost layers and cake with green frosting then, using a rose tip attached to a piping bag filled with yellow frosting, pipe flowers accross top of cake.

Approximate servings per recipe: 12. Per frosted serving: Calories 630; Fat 21g; Sodium 306mg; Carbohydrate 106g; Fiber 1g; Sugars 74g; Protein 7g.

Great Cakes Alive!

You Take the Cake!

Good things do take time, but its time well spent when it goes into making this fabulously fluffy, Cool 'n' Creamy Coconut Layer Cake!

Food That Makes You Feel Good!

Cool 'n' Creamy Coconut Layer Cake

2 3/4 cups all purpose flour
1 teaspoon baking powder
1/2 teaspoon baking soda
1/2 teaspoon salt
1 3/4 cups granulated sugar
1 cup unsalted butter, room temperature
1 cup canned cream of coconut *See note below
4 large eggs, separated and at room temperature
1 teaspoon pure vanilla extract
1 cup well shaken buttermilk
pinch of salt

FROSTING
16 ounces cream cheese, room temperature
1/2 cup butter, room temperature
2 cups powdered sugar
1/2 cup canned cream of coconut
1 teaspoon pure vanilla extract
4 cups sweetened flaked coconut

Preheat oven to 350 degrees. Butter and flour two 9 inch cake pans with 2 inch high sides or three 8 inch diameter cake pans with 2 inch high sides. In a medium bowl, whisk flour, baking powder, baking soda and salt to blend. In a large bowl of a mixer, beat sugar, butter and cream of coconut until fluffy. Beat in egg yolks and vanilla. On low speed, mix in dry ingredients and buttermilk alternately just until blended. Do not over beat. In another medium mixing bowl, use clean, dry beaters to beat egg whites and a pinch of salt until whites are stiff like meringue, but not dry. Carefully fold egg whites into batter then divide cake batter between prepared pans. Bake cakes until tester inserted into center comes out clean, about 30 to 45 minutes.
FROSTING: Beat cream cheese in medium bowl until fluffy. Add butter and beat to blend. Add sugar, cream of coconut and vanilla and beat until well blended. Cool cakes in pans on rack 10 minutes then run a sharp knife around edges to loosen cakes before turning out onto racks to cool completely. When cooled, place one layer on cake plate, spread 1/2 to 3/4 cup of frosting over layer then sprinkle with shredded coconut and repeat until all layers are assembled. Frost top and sides of cake and sprinkle with coconut, gently pressing into sides to adhere. Cover with plastic wrap and refrigerate. * Note: Do not substitute coconut milk.

Approximate servings per recipe: 24. Per serving: Calories 443; Fat 17g; Sodium 210mg; Carbohydrate 43g; Fiber 1g; Sugars 29g; Protein 4g.

Great Cakes Alive!

A flourless cake isn't just for those who are gluten intolerant, at least not when it comes to chocolate. The absence of flour allows the chocolate flavor to breathe through every bite of this delicious delight, so dig in!

Food That Makes You Feel Good!

Flourless Chocolate Cake
Butter and cocoa for pan
parchment or wax paper
8 ounces unsweetened chocolate
1 cup butter
1 cup unsweetened cocoa powder
1 1/2 cups granulated sugar
6 large eggs
6 tablespoons strong cold coffee or coffee liqueur

Preheat oven to 325 degrees. Butter two 8 inch round cake pans and line the bottom of the pans with parchment or wax paper. Butter the paper. Lightly dust pan with cocoa and tap out excess. Melt chocolate squares and butter in microwave. In a medium bowl, combine cocoa, sugar and eggs. Add the coffee or liqueur then whisk in the melted chocolate mixture. Batter should have a cookie dough type consistency. Divide equally and spread batter into prepared pans. Bake for 35 minutes or until a tester comes out clean. Cool cake in pan for 1 hour. Turn out and carefully peel paper off the bottom of the cake. Refrigerate until cold. Frost between layers then top and sides of cake with Chocolate Butter Cream Frosting. Return Cake to refrigerator to chill. Serve cold.

Approximate servings per recipe: 16. Per serving: Calories 206; Fat 11g; Carbohydrates 26g; Fiber 2g; Protein 3g.

Chocolate Frosting
2/3 cup butter, softened
1/3 cup unsweetened cocoa powder, sifted
4 cups powdered sugar, sifted
1/3 cup half and half - more or less, as needed
1 teaspoon pure vanilla extract

In the bowl of an electric mixer, cream butter, about 5 minutes. Stir in cocoa powder, powdered sugar, vanilla then half and half. Beat until desired texture is achieved.

Approximate servings per recipe: 24. Per serving: Calories 103; Fat 5g; Sodium 29mg; Carbohydrate 16g; Fiber 2g; Sugars 13g; Protein 1g.

Great Cakes Alive!

Food That Makes You Feel Good!

Tangerine Dream Cake
CAKE
2 tangerines
1 packet of unsweetened orange drink mix
1 box lemon cake mix, batter prepared

GLAZE
1 cup water
2 3 ounce boxes orange gelatin, divided use
1 cup fresh tangerine juice

FROSTING
1 3.5 ounce box vanilla instant pudding
1 cup milk
1 teaspoon pure vanilla extract
8 ounces non-dairy whipped topping, thawed

CAKE: Using the fine shred side of a box grater, grate the rind from tangerines. In an electric mixer bowl, prepare cake mix according to box instructions then stir in rind and packet of orange drink mix. Pour batter into a greased 9x13 inch cake pan and bake according to cake box instructions.
GLAZE: Meanwhile, in a small saucepan, heat 1 cup of water to a boil. Add one 3 ounce box of orange gelatin powder, stirring until gelatin is completely dissolved. Mix in the tangerine juice and place in refrigerator to cool down, but not solidify.
When the cake has finished baking but while it is still hot, use a toothpick to punch dozens of holes throughout the entire top of the cake. Let cake cool for 10 minutes then pour the prepared liquid gelatin mixture evenly over the top of cake. Refrigerate cake for 1 hour.
FROSTING: With a mixer, beat together remaining box of orange gelatin, instant pudding, milk, and vanilla extract. Beat for two full minutes. Fold non-dairy whipped topping into mixture then spread evenly over top of cake. Refrigerate cake for at least one hour before serving. Keep cake refrigerated.

Approximate servings per recipe: 24. Per serving: Calories 140; Fat 2g; Carbohydrates 19g; Protein 4g.

Great Cakes Alive!

Food That Makes You Feel Good!

Incredible Carrot Cake

2 cups all purpose flour
2 teaspoons baking soda
1 teaspoon baking powder
1 teaspoon salt
2 teaspoons ground cinnamon
1 3/4 cups granulated sugar
1 cup vegetable oil
3 large eggs
1 teaspoon pure vanilla extract
2 cups shredded carrots
1 cup sweetened flaked coconut
1 cup chopped walnuts
8 ounces crushed pineapple, drained

FROSTING
8 ounces cream cheese, softened
1/4 cup butter, softened
2 cups powdered sugar
1 teaspoon pure vanilla extract

Preheat oven to 350 degrees. Butter and flour two 9 inch diameter cake pans with 2 inch high sides, or three 8 inch diameter cake pans with 2 inch high sides, or a 9x13x2 inch pan. In a large mixing bowl, mix flour, baking soda, baking powder, salt, cinnamon and sugar. Make a well in the center and add oil, eggs and vanilla.
Using a wooden spoon, mix until smooth then stir in carrots, coconut, walnuts and pineapple. Pour into prepared pan of choice and bake cake(s) until tester inserted into center comes out clean, 30 to 45 minutes.
FROSTING: In the bowl of an electric mixer, beat cream cheese and butter until smooth, about 5 minutes, then add powdered sugar and vanilla and beat until creamy. Allow cake to cool for 10 minutes before removing from pan(s). When cooled, frost cake.

Approximate servings per recipe: 12. Per serving: Calories 564; Fat 38g; Sodium 564mg; Carbohydrate 68g; Fiber 2g; Sugars 55g; Protein 7g.

Great Cakes Alive!

Pineapple Upside Down Cake

1/2 cup butter
1 cup dark brown sugar, packed
1 (20 ounce) can sliced pineapple
6 maraschino cherries, cut in half lengthwise
1 (18 ounce) package pineapple cake mix
1 (4 ounce) box vanilla instant pudding mix
1 cup pineapple juice
1/2 cup canola oil
4 eggs

Preheat oven to 325 degrees. Melt butter in a 9"x13" pan in oven. Sprinkle brown sugar evenly over butter in pan. Drain canned pineapple into a measuring cup. Place pineapple slices evenly accross botton of pan, cutting the last two in half to cover pan.

Place maraschino cherry halves in the center of the pineapple slices, cut side up.
In a large mixing bowl, combine cake mix, pudding mix, pineapple juice, oil and eggs.
Stir on slow speed for 30 seconds then beat on medium speed for 2 minutes. Pour batter into pan over fruit then bake for 45 to 55 minutes, or until a toothpick comes out clean.
Cool for 5 minutes then turn cake out onto a serving platter, pineapple side up.

Approximate servings per recipe: 12. Calories 316; Fat 18g;
Sodium 221mg; Carbohydrate 37g; Fiber 1g; Sugars 34g; Protein 2g.

Food That Makes You Feel Good!

Texas Sheet Cake

2 cups all-purpose flour
2 cups granulated sugar
1/2 teaspoon baking soda
1/2 teaspoon salt
2 large eggs plus 2 yolks
2 teaspoons pure vanilla extract
1/4 cup sour cream
8 ounces semisweet chocolate, chopped
4 tablespoons unsalted butter
3/4 cup vegetable oil
3/4 cup water
1/2 cup Dutch-processed cocoa powder

FROSTING
8 tablespoons unsalted butter
1/2 cup heavy cream
1/2 cup Dutch-processed cocoa powder
1 tablespoon light corn syrup
3 cups powdered sugar
1 tablespoon pure vanilla extract
1 cup toasted pecans, chopped

CAKE: Adjust oven rack to middle position and heat oven to 350 degrees. Grease 18"x13" rimmed baking sheet. Combine flour, sugar, baking soda, and salt in large bowl.
Whisk eggs and yolks, vanilla, and sour cream in another bowl until smooth.
Heat chocolate, butter, oil, water, and cocoa in large saucepan over medium heat, stirring occasionally, until smooth, 3 to 5 minutes. Whisk chocolate mixture into flour mixture until incorporated. Whisk egg mixture into batter, then pour into prepared baking pan. Bake until toothpick inserted into center comes out clean, 18 to 20 minutes. Transfer to wire rack.
FROSTING: About 5 minutes before cake is done, heat butter, cream, cocoa, and corn syrup in large saucepan over medium heat, stirring occasionally, until smooth. Off heat, whisk in confectioners' sugar and vanilla. Spread warm icing evenly over hot cake and sprinkle with pecans. Let cake cool to room temperature on wire rack, about 1 hour, then refrigerate until icing is set, about 1 hour longer. (Cake can be wrapped in plastic and refrigerated for up to 2 days. Bring to room temperature before serving.)
Cut into 3-inch squares. Serve.

Approximate servings per recipe: 24. Per serving: Calories 315; Fat 9g; Sodium 263mg; Carbohydrate 27g; Fiber 0.5g; Sugars 29g; Protein 3g.

Great Cakes Alive!

Food That Makes You Feel Good!

Tennessee Stack Cake

FILLING
8 apples, peeled, cored and sliced
1 cup packed dark brown sugar
1 1/2 teaspoons ground cinnamon
1/2 teaspoon ground cloves
1/2 teaspoon ground allspice

CAKE
6 cups all purpose flour
1 tablespoon baking powder
1 teaspoon baking soda
1/4 teaspoon salt
1/2 cup well shaken buttermilk
2 large eggs
1 teaspoon pure vanilla extract
1 cup butter, softened
2 cups cane sugar
Powdered sugar and cinnamon for dusting

FILLING: In a medium saucepan, bring apples to a boil. Reduce heat and simmer until apples are soft, about 10 minutes. Let apples cool until just warm, about 15 minutes, then puree in a food processor until smooth. Add brown sugar, cinnamon, cloves, and allspice and blend until fully mixed.
CAKE: Preheat oven to 350 degrees. Place two oven racks in the upper-middle and lower-middle positions. Coat two cookie sheets with cooking spray. In a medium bowl whisk flour, baking powder, baking soda and salt. In a large measuring cup, whisk buttermilk, eggs and vanilla. In a large bowl of an electric mixer, at medium-high speed, beat butter and cane sugar until fluffy, about 2 minutes. Scrape bowl down if necessary. Alternately, - in two batches - add flour mixture and buttermilk mixture, beating after each addition and scraping down the bowl as needed. Dough will be thick. Divide the dough into 8 equal portions. Working with 2 portions at a time on a lightly floured surface, roll each out into a 10-inch circle about 1/4 inch thick. Using a 9 inch cake pan as a template, trim away the excess dough to form two perfectly round 9 inch disks. Transfer disks to prepared baking sheets and bake 10 to 12 minutes or until golden brown, rotating and switching the baking sheets halfway through baking time. Transfer disks to a rack to cool completely, at least 1 hour. Repeat with the remaining dough. Place one cake layer on a serving plate and spread with 1 cup filling. Repeat 6 times. Top with the final layer, wrap tightly in plastic and refrigerate until the layers soften, at least 24 hours or up to 2 days. Dust with powdered sugar and cinnamon before serving.

Approximate servings per recipe: 16. Per serving: Calories 442; Fat 13g; Sodium 233 mg; Carbohydrates 76g; Fiber 2g; Sugar 39g; Protein 6g.

Great Cakes Alive!

The Mardi Gras King Cake is well known for its tradition of having a prize - a doll, coin or bean - tucked inside. The person who finds the prize is not only crowned "king" and blessed with a full year of good fortune but also, as luck would have it, be responsible for buying the cake and throwing the party next year!

Food That Makes You Feel Good!

Nowhere else in America is Fat Tuesday celebrated with such zest and to its legal limit like it is in New Orleans. Even a hurricane the size of Katrina could not stop this city from continuing its cultural institution known simply as Mardi Gras.

Called Mardi Gras, Le Carnival, Pancake Tuesday, Shrove Tuesday, or even Fetter Dienstag, this day is intended for us to clear our homes of all fat, eggs and dairy products to make it easier for us to fast during Lent, and what better way than to have one last, big food hurrah?

Mardi Gras is known for its food and one of the most popular items on any Mardi Gras menu is the King Cake.

Believed to have been brought to New Orleans from France circa 1870, hundreds of thousands of King Cakes are consumed at celebrations every year. In fact, no Mardi Gras party would be considered complete without one!

This delicious cake is really more of a cross between a coffee ring and a sweet bread, and through the years its fillings have become as varied and elaborate as the day it is made for. However, one thing that has never changed about the King Cake are its colors - purple for justice, green for faith and gold for power - all represented in true Mardi Gras fashion.

Part of the King Cake tradition is to have a treasure hidden inside the cake, usually a small doll, a coin or a bean. The person who finds the hidden treasure is crowned "king" and blessed with a year's worth of good fortune. But, as king they are also bound by custom to host next year's party and to provide a new King Cake as well!

If you can't make it to the Vieux Carre in the French Quarter of New Orleans to experience Mardi Gras in person, you can just as easily make a King Cake of your own either from scratch or a convenient kit offered by reputable flour and baking supply companies.

Recipes for King Cakes do vary and can have lots of steps, but don't be intimidated by them. None of the steps are difficult, they just take a little time.

Don't forget to slip a doll or a coin or a bean inside the cake, too and, be sure to do it after baking it and from the underside so that no one can tell where it is hidden. Also be sure to tell everyone to inspect their piece before biting into it to avoid any dental or choking hazards and lawsuits!

Here are some deliciously different King Cake recipes that are diverse enough to accommodate even the tightest of schedules.

" Laissez les bons temps rouler!"
(Let the good times roll!)

Mardi Gras King Cake

1 1/4 ounce package active dry yeast
1/4 cup warm water
1/2 cup warm milk
1/2 cup granulated sugar
1/2 cup butter, melted
1/2 teaspoon salt
3 large eggs, beaten
3 to 4 cups all purpose flour
6 ounce almond filling /paste

GARNISH
3/4 cup sugar, divided into 3 parts
Food coloring: gold, purple and green
Tiny plastic doll, coin or dried bean

ICING
1 1/2 cups powdered sugar
3 tablespoons butter
1 tablespoon milk
1 tablespoon pure vanilla extract

Combine yeast and water in a small bowl, stirring until dissolved. Set aside until yeast is proofed, 10 to 15 minutes. In a large mixing bowl combine the milk, sugar, and butter, stirring until sugar is dissolved. Add the salt, eggs, and yeast mixture and blend thoroughly. Beat in 1 1/2 cups of flour to make a smooth batter. Add additional flour to make a soft dough (dough will be very sticky). With a standing mixer and dough hook, knead dough approximately 8 minutes or until smooth and elastic. Shape dough into a ball and place in a buttered bowl, turning to lightly coat top with some of the butter. Cover loosely with plastic wrap and let rise until doubled. Punch down the dough and flatten into a long oval. Spread almond filling on oval and roll into a rope. Join ends together leaving large oval hole in the middle. Cover and let rise until double, about 1 hour. While the bread is rising, preheat oven to 350 degrees. Bake ring for 30 minutes in the preheated oven or until golden brown and sounds hollow when thumped. Remove and let cool on wire rack. Place a plastic doll, coin or bean into oval from underneath.

GARNISH: Divide sugar into 3 equal parts then place in 3 sealable plastic bags and zip closed. Knead each bag gently to break up any lumps in sugar then open bag and add 3 to 4 drops of food coloring spaced around the interior of the bag. Close bag and knead gently but thoroughly until color is distributed evenly throughout sugar. Note: The color purple is achieved by combining blue and red.

ICING: In a small bowl, combine powdered sugar, butter, milk and vanilla. Beat until fluffy. Frost cooled cake with icing then sprinkle top of cake with colored sugar, alternating the three colors.

Approximate servings per recipe: 14.
Per serving: Calories 419; Fat 18g; Carbohydrates 56g; Fiber 1g; Sugars 31g; Protein 7g.

Food That Makes You Feel Good!

Quick 'n' Easy King Cake
1 12 ounce can crescent rolls
1/8 cup ground cinnamon
1/4 cup butter, softened
1 21 ounce can fruit pie filling
1 8 ounce package cream cheese, softened
1 cup powdered sugar

ICING
1 cup powdered sugar
1 tablespoon fresh lemon juice
1 tablespoon water

GARNISH
3/4 cup sugar, divided into 3 parts
Food coloring: gold, purple and green
Tiny plastic doll, coin or dried bean

Preheat oven to 350 degrees. Open can of crescent rolls and unroll in one piece. With your fingers, press seams together to form one piece of dough. Combine butter and cinnamon then gently spread evenly over the dough. In a bowl, combine cream cheese and powdered sugar then drop by teaspoonful randomly across the top of the dough. Drop pie filling by teaspoonful randomly across the dough as you did the cream cheese. Starting on the wide end, carefully roll dough like a jelly roll so filling is inside. Place on baking pan with seam side down and form into a circle, pinching the ends together. Bake at 350 for 15 to 20 minutes or until golden brown.
GARNISH: Divide sugar into 3 equal parts then place in 3 sealable plastic bags and zip closed. Knead each bag gently to break up any lumps in sugar then open bag and add 3 to 4 drops of food coloring spaced around the interior of the bag. Close bag and knead gently but thoroughly until color is distributed evenly throughout sugar.
Note: The color purple is achieved by combining blue and red.
ICING: In a small bowl, combine powdered sugar, lemon juice and water. Stir until smooth. When cake is cool, insert plastic doll, coin or bean randomly into the bottom of the cake. Pour icing over the top of the cake. Sprinkle top of cake with colored sugar, alternating the three colors.

Approximate servings per recipe: 8. Per serving: Calories 460; Fat 18g; Carbohydrate 60g; Fiber 3g; Sugars 40g; Protein 6g.

Great Cakes Alive!

Food That Makes You Feel Good!

New Orleans style King Cake

FILLING
1/4 cup dark brown sugar, packed
3/8 cup granulated sugar
1/2 teaspoon cinnamon

TOPPING
1/2 cup granulated sugar
gold, purple, and green food coloring

CAKE
1/2 cup plus 1/2 teaspoon butter
1/3 cup fat-free evaporated milk
1/4 cup granulated sugar
1 teaspoon salt
1 tablespoon sugar
1 package dry yeast
1/4 cup warm water
2 large eggs
1/2 teaspoon grated fresh lemon rind
1 teaspoon grated fresh orange rind
3 cups all purpose flour
1/2 cup butter, melted
1 large egg, beaten

GARNISH
Tiny plastic doll, coin or dried bean

FILLING: Mix the 1/4 cup brown sugar and 3/8 cup granulated sugar and the cinnamon and set aside.

TOPPING: Divide sugar into 3 equal parts then place in 3 sealable plastic bags and zip closed. Knead each bag gently to break up any lumps in sugar then open bag and add 3 to 4 drops of food coloring spaced around the interior of the bag. Close bag and knead gently but thoroughly until color is distributed evenly throughout sugar. Note: The color purple is achieved by combining blue and red. Set aside.

CAKE: Melt butter, milk, 1/4 cup sugar and salt. Cool to lukewarm. In a large mixing bowl, combine sugar, yeast and water. Let stand until foaming, about 5 to 10 minutes. Beat eggs into the yeast mixture. Add the milk mixture and the lemon and orange rinds. Stir in the flour, about 1/4 cup at a time. Knead dough until smooth, 5 to 10 minutes.
Place dough in a large greased mixing bowl, turning dough to grease the top. Cover and let rise until doubled. When the dough has doubled, punch it down.
Roll into a 30x15 inch rectangle, brush with melted butter then cut into 3 long strips. Sprinkle filling on the strips, leaving a 1" length-wise edge plain for sealing.
Roll each strip lengthwise toward the center and seal edge to create 3 filled ropes. Braid ropes into a closed circle. Place cake on a large baking sheet and cover. Let rise until doubled. Preheat oven to 350 degrees. Brush cake with beaten egg. Sprinkle top with colored sugars in a creative, crisscross fashion. Bake for 20 minutes. Remove from pan while still hot. Place doll, coin or dried bean in the underside of the cake.

Approximate servings per recipe: 8.
Per serving: Calories 450; Fat 14g; Carbohydrate 70g; Fiber 1g; Sugars 36g; Protein 8g.

Heaven Scent

Do you have any angels in your life? Show them you care by making them an angel food cake. It is truly a cake that lives up to its name.

Food That Makes You Feel Good!

They say that many of us wander through life without ever really getting to know anyone, without ever solidly connecting with another human being. What's worse, they say that we're the ones to blame! It's our fault we don't make an effort to be a more positive presence in the lives of others.

That could never be said about my friend and colleague, Diane Moshier, for she was a woman as hot as apple pie, and I do mean that literally!

From the day I first met her, which was while sitting shoulder-to-shoulder at my first planning session in the Sturgis Journal's conference room, Diane was heating up the place. In fact, the first thing she ever said to me, and in a hurried tone was, "Hi. I'm Diane Moshier and I'm about to have a hot flash so you may want to scoot your chair away from me. I wouldn't want to drip on you." I smiled and said, "It's okay. It won't be the first time something dripped on me." We both burst into a laugh then quickly returned our attention to the meeting.

I didn't know it then, but it was the beginning of a running conversation I would have with Diane that would last - off and on - over what would become the last 8 years of her life.

Diane loved to catch me at the most inopportune moments. One time I was rushing out of the meat market and without uttering a single word Diane snatched my grocery bag right out of my hand, then peering into it snapped, "What's the food lady cooking tonight?" Tipping her head sideways she muttered, "Bologna? Miss Vitality Cuisine is making bologna for dinner?" "Yup" I said.

"Hmmm" she mused as she closed the bag and handed it back to me. "Tell me, Miss Kurella. Should I be on the lookout for a bologna recipe in a future column?" "No!" I said smiling. "Some recipes are so special they shouldn't be published." "You got that right, sister!" she chirped. Then off she went!

Diane was a bright light you rarely find here on earth and her brilliance glowed even brighter when her battle with the "alien" descended upon her.

A Cancer diagnosis makes many people not want to get out of bed. For Diane it did the opposite- she took a dream vacation to Mexico!

After being severely weakened by disease, Diane's capacity to be a continued source of strength, courage and humor to her readers never seemed to diminish.

Her ability to reach outside of herself, through her pain and misery, to lift others up while in the midst of her own dark and difficult struggle cannot help but leave me - leave all of us - with a legacy of hope that it is indeed possible to find happiness even in the darkest days of our lives, if we so choose.

I will never forget the warm, loving glow she never failed to pour into her life and into her column and in turn, into the lives of anyone who ever read her.

Diane taught me the importance of connecting with others and that in order to feel love you must first love others. That said, if ever you need to feel love, take Diane Moshier's approach to life. Make something special and share it with someone you love.

Great Cakes Alive!

Food That Makes You Feel Good!

Awesome Angel Food Cake
1 cup cake flour
3/4 cup plus 2 tablespoons granulated sugar
2 teaspoons pure vanilla extract
1/2 teaspoon almond extract
12 large egg whites
2 teaspoons cream of tartar
1/2 teaspoon sea salt
3/4 cup granulated sugar
Dark Chocolate Glaze (optional)

Heat oven to 375 degrees. In a medium bowl, sift together cake flour with 3/4 cup and 2 tablespoons of sugar; set aside. Combine vanilla and almond extracts in a small bowl and set aside. With a mixer, beat egg whites, cream of tartar, and salt until it forms peaks. Add the remaining 3/4 cup of sugar slowly. Beat on high until stiff peaks form. Set mixer to low and slowly add flour mixture and extracts alternately. Spoon into an angel food cake pan. Use a knife to move through batter to remove any air pockets. Bake 30 to 35 minutes or until top springs back when touched lightly. Invert pan onto a soda bottle or funnel to cool completely.

Approximate servings per recipe: 16. Per serving: Calories 123; Fat 0.1g; Carbohydrates 27g; Fiber 0.11g; Protein 4g.

Dark Chocolate Glaze
4 tablespoons unsweetened cocoa powder
3 tablespoons butter
1 1/2 cups powdered sugar
3 to 4 tablespoons water
1 teaspoon pure vanilla extract

In a small saucepan, under low heat, melt chocolate and butter, stirring until smooth. Remove from heat and stir in powdered sugar, alternately with water, until desired consistency is reached. Stir in vanilla extract.

Approximate servings per recipe: 16. Per serving: Calories 66; Fat 2g; Carbohydrates 12g; Fiber 0g; Protein 0g.

Great Cakes Alive!

56

Food That Makes You Feel Good!

Fantasy on a Fork

2 pounds strawberries, divided use
2/3 cup granulated sugar
1 10 ounce angel food cake
8 ounces non-dairy whipped topping, thawed

Thinly slice one pound of the strawberries into a medium bowl. Combine with sugar, cover, and let sweat at room temperature for 2 to 4 hours, or overnight in the refrigerator. Slice angel food cake in half horizontally to form two layers. Place bottom layer on a serving plate and cover evenly with all the sweated strawberries. Evenly spread whipped topping over strawberry layer. Set the top cake layer on top of the whipped topping. Cover top and sides of cake with whipped topping. Slice remaining strawberries and use to decorate cake any way you like.

Approximate servings per recipe: 16. Per serving: Calories 243; Fat 2g; Carbohydrates 27g; Fiber 2g; Protein 2g.

Great Cakes Alive!

Petite Pleasures

Food That Makes You Feel Good!

Ah, Valentines Day! Soft and sweet as a rose when you're in love, quite prickly when you're not!

At this point in my life, which is about half way through, I've had my fair share of both and I for one, definitely prefer its softer side.

I was foolish enough to make that date an anniversary, which now as an ex causes me to reflect on all my life failures whenever this date rolls around - not good!

I wondered just how many other fools - like me - have made this day more important than it should be, so I decided to ask around and I found that thoughts tend to run right down gender lines.

Many women expressed the same thoughts as a 23-year-old newly married bride who finds this day to be, "A day to love! The roses and love letter my husband gives me makes up for the entire year!"

Then there were men, with a good majority expressing the same sentiment of a 28-year-old male, who called the day, "A secular holiday built on sucking the life and love out of all men on earth!"

Personally, I am a hopeless romantic. I am in love with love and like so many who find themselves returning to the dating scene in midlife, I have found that hopeful romantic moments tend to be disappointing only because the reality of them can never measure up to the impossible fantasy that marketing and advertising have built up so strongly in our weak, vunerable minds.

In the end, perhaps John Lennon put it best when he wrote, "All we need is love."

If by chance you find yourself Valentine-less on this day, do what I do. Be a little bit nicer to yourself and repeat this little verse: "Roses may be red and heartbreak may be blue, but a dessert will always be the sweetest thing - through and through!"

Make Valentines Day an empowering one. Be your own Valentine and treat yourself to a swift, single-sized sweet made just for you!

Here are some special petite pleasures designed to help make this day a sweet one, whether flying solo or with someone else!

Petite Caramel Pecan Cakes

1/2 cup granulated sugar
6 tablespoons water, divided use
5 tablespoons all purpose flour
1/8 teaspoon baking soda
1/8 teaspoon salt
1 tablespoon granulated sugar
1 tablespoon brown sugar, packed
1 tablespoon unsalted butter, melted
1 large egg, beaten
1 tablespoon heavy whipping cream
2 tablespoons pecans, toasted

In a small, heavy saucepan over medium heat, combine 1/2 cup sugar and 2 tablespoons of water, stirring until sugar dissolves. Bring to a boil, stirring occasionally until it develops the color of maple syrup, about 10 minutes. Meanwhile, in a small bowl, combine flour, baking soda, salt, and tablespoon of sugar and brown sugar, blending well. Set aside. When color develops in sugar and water mixture, remove from heat. Carefully stir in remaining 4 tablespoons of water. Mixture will steam vigorously and may stiffen. Return to a boil and stir until mixture is smooth then simmer until just syrupy, about 3 minutes. Cool to room temperature before proceeding. Measure off 2 tablespoons of cooled caramel syrup into a small container and set aside for garnish. In a 2 cup measure, place 1 tablespoon butter and cook in the microwave on high for 30 seconds or until melted. To the butter, whisk in the beaten egg and 1 tablespoon of cream, blending well. Add the remaining caramel syrup then gradually blend in the bowl of dry ingredients until smooth. Fold in pecans. Cover and chill at least 12 hours or overnight. Place a rack in the center of the oven and preheat to 325 degrees. Butter and lightly flour 2 1/2 cup ramekins or cups. Cut a round of parchment paper to fit in bottom of each cup. Divide batter between cups. Bake for 30 minutes. Cool cakes to warm. Reheat the reserved 2 tablespoons of caramel syrup in microwave on high for 15 to 30 seconds. Invert cakes onto plates, peel off parchment and spoon warm caramel syrup on top just before serving.

Approximate servings per recipe: 2. Per serving: Calories 456; Fat 15g; Sodium 91mg; Carbohydrate 79g; Fiber 1g; Sugars 63g; Protein 4g.

Food That Makes You Feel Good!

Luscious Little Lemon Cakes

1/2 cup all purpose flour
1 teaspoon baking powder
1/8 teaspoon salt
3 tablespoons plain yogurt
1/4 teaspoon pure vanilla extract
1 tablespoon freshly squeezed lemon juice
1/4 teaspoon finely grated lemon rind
3 tablespoon butter
1/3 cup granulated sugar
1 large egg

ICING
1/2 cup powdered sugar
1/2 to 1 teaspoon milk
1 teaspoon freshly squeezed lemon juice

Preheat oven to 350 degrees. In a bowl, combine flour, baking powder and salt.
In a small bowl, combine yogurt, vanilla, lemon juice and rind, mixing well.
In a glass 2 cup measure, cream butter and 1/3 cup granulated sugar until light, about 5 minutes. Add egg, beating well, then add half of the flour mixture and half of the yogurt mixture, blending well. Add remaining flour and yogurt mixtures, and beat until smooth. Divide evenly between 2 buttered and floured 1/2 cup ramekins or cups. Bake until a toothpick inserted in center comes out clean, about 20 minutes.
Cool in pan for 10 minutes then invert onto a rack and cool completely.
ICING: In a 1 cup measure, combine powdered sugar with lemon juice and milk, adding enough milk so that it's slightly runny, stirring until smooth. Pour over cakes.
Let cakes stand for 30 minutes before serving.

Approximate servings per recipe: 2. Per serving: Calories 615; Fat 17g; Sodium 397 mg; Carbohydrates 81g; Fiber 1g; Sugar 1g; Protein 7g.

Rich Rewards

Make Valentines Day an empowering one - be your own Valentine and treat yourself to one of life's many petite pleasures like this ultra elegant yet easy to make Molten Lava Cake. And, don't be fooled by its small size. One portion is so rich and rewarding it's guaranteed to satisfy!

Food That Makes You Feel Good!

Marvelous Mini Molten Lava Cakes

4 tablespoons bittersweet chocolate chips
2 tablespoons semisweet chocolate chips
3 tablespoons butter
1 teaspoon butter
3 tablespoons all purpose flour
1/2 cup powdered sugar
1 large egg
1 large egg yolk
1/2 teaspoon pure vanilla extract
2 teaspoons Grand Marnier (optional)

GARNISH (optional)
powdered sugar
raspberries

Preheat oven to 400 degrees. Grease 4 1/2 cup ramekins or cups.
In a glass 2 cup measure, place both types of chocolate chips and butter and microwave for 1 minute. Stir well. Blend in flour. Add sugar and stir well.
It will become stiff. Blend in egg until smooth then add egg yoke, stirring until smooth. Stir in vanilla and Grand Marnier, if using and blend until smooth.
Divide batter evenly between cups. Bake for 8 minutes. Edges should be firm but the center will be runny. Run a knife around the edge to loosen.
Invert onto dessert plates.
GARNISH: Sprinkle with powdered sugar and fresh raspberries,
if desired.

Approximate servings per recipe: 4. Per serving: Calories 334; Fat 19g; Sodium 23 mg; Carbohydrates 32; Fiber 3g; Sugar 25g; Protein 10g.

Great Cakes Alive!

Food That Makes You Feel Good!

One of the big upsides to summers in the north is being able to put the snow shovel away for awhile. The downside is having to turn the oven off, which in my house is left on all winter to keep the chill out of the kitchen and offer a "running" excuse for baking something yummy all winter long!

So what's a northerner to do when it's hot outside but they still feel like baking? I say bake something quick, like a cup cake!

In the 19th century, the term cup cake didn't refer to what we know and love today. Rather, it was first used in cooking to describe a recipe style. More specifically, that a recipe called for ingredients to be measured out in cups rather than be weighed out.

Weighing ingredients had been the traditional custom of the day so when the idea of measuring in volume instead of weight was introduced it was considered revolutionary and, according to "Baking in America" by Greg Patent, widely embraced because of the tremendous time it could save in the kitchen.

The use of the cup cake then created what was coined the number cake, which was dubbed so because it used a mnemonic device for remembering a recipe: One cup of butter, two cups of sugar, three cups of flour and four eggs plus one cup of milk and one spoonful of soda. This formula also became known as the one-two-three-four cake.

At the turn of the 20th century, cup cake took on a yet another meaning. That's when the practice of baking in small containers - cupcakes as we know them today – finally came into being.

Cooking in cups was born purely out of convenience. Hearth ovens took a long time to bake those early, enormous cakes and those long baking times meant many a burnt cake.

When gem pans (muffin pans) were first introduced in the early 1900's, the idea took off like a shot and the desire to bake cupcakes has never waned since.

Today, pan manufacturers are continually thinking up new ways for us to enjoy this tiny treat, offering us all kinds of specialty pans that can make a new array of even smaller-baked treats like super mini cupcake pan and the more bizarre muffin top pan designed to render more of a cookie than cake out of batter - a clear indication that even in the modern world, the old fashion flavor of a cupcake will never get old!

A nice feature of the cupcake is that it can be can be frosted and frozen individually and, being tiny in size means little freezer space, offering you a self-service bakery right at your own fingertips!

Here are a few fabulous recipes that are filled with so much flavor you just may think twice about ever baking a whole cake again!

Great Cakes Alive!

These Coconut Key Lime Cupcakes may be little in size but they are big on flavor and perfect for when you want a little something sweet.

Food That Makes You Feel Good!

Coconut Key Lime Cupcakes

1 3/4 cups all purpose flour
2 teaspoons baking powder
1/2 teaspoon fine sea salt
3 large egg whites
3/4 cup whole milk
1 tablespoon key lime juice
3/4 cup granulated sugar
1/2 cup butter, softened
1 cup shredded sweetened coconut

FROSTING
8 ounces cream cheese, softened
1/2 cup butter, softened
2 ounces white chocolate chips, melted
1/4 cup key lime juice
2 cups powdered sugar
1 cup shredded sweetened coconut

Preheat the oven to 325 degrees. Line 12 regular size muffin tin cups with paper liners. In a large bowl, sift together flour, baking powder and salt. In a large measuring cup, combine egg whites, milk and key lime juice. In the bowl of an electric mixer fitted with a paddle attachment, cream butter and sugar until light and fluffy, about 5 minutes. Then, with the mixer running on low, add the egg mixture while alternately adding the dry ingredients, beginning and ending with the dry. Mix until just combined.
Fold in 1 cup coconut. Fill each muffin tin cup 3/4 full with batter. Bake for 25 to 35 minutes, until the tops are light brown and a toothpick tester comes out clean.
Allow to cool in the pan for 15 minutes. Remove to a rack and cool completely.
FROSTING: in the bowl of an electric mixer fitted with a paddle attachment, beat together cream cheese, butter, melted chocolate chips and key lime juice. Add the powdered sugar and mix until smooth. Frost cupcakes and sprinkle with the coconut.

Approximate servings per recipe: 24. Per serving: Calories 270; Fat 14g; Carbohydrates 35g; Fiber 1g; Sugar 26g; Protein 3g.

Great Cakes Alive!

Pumpkin Pinkies offer all the big flavors of pumpkin packed into a tiny little snack.

Food That Makes You Feel Good!

Pumpkin Pinkies
1 3/4 cups all purpose flour
1 teaspoon baking soda
1/4 teaspoon ground ginger
1 1/2 teaspoons ground cinnamon
1 1/2 teaspoons grated nutmeg
1/2 teaspoon salt
1 1/2 cups granulated sugar
1/3 cup water
2 large eggs
1/2 cup canola oil
1 cup solid pack pumpkin

Preheat oven to 350 degrees. Spray 24 miniature muffin tins with nonstick cooking spray.
In a large bowl, combine all dry ingredients, mixing well. In a medium bowl, combine all wet ingredients and mix well. Pour wet mixture into dry mixture. Mix well. Fill each tin 3/4 full. Bake for 10 minutes.

Approximate servings per recipe: 12. Per serving: Calories 226; Fat 6g; Carbohydrates 41g; Fiber 1g; Protein 3g.

Pecan Praline Pinkies
1 cup chopped pecans
1/2 cup all purpose flour
1 cup packed brown sugar
2/3 cup butter, melted
2 large eggs

Preheat oven to 350 degrees. In a large bowl, combine all ingredients and mix well. Spray 24 miniature muffin tins with nonstick cooking spray. Fill each cup 3/4 full. Bake for 18 minutes or until toothpick tester comes out clean.

Approximate servings per recipe: 24. Per serving: Calories 126; Fat 9g; Carbohydrates 11g; Fiber 0.5g; Sugar 9g; Protein 1g.

Pies & Cheesecakes

Easy as Pie!

Food That Makes You Feel Good!

Making a delicious pie crust has never been easier!

It is rare for a person not to enjoy a pleasing slice of home-baked pie, but while pies from scratch are healthier than their old and over processed counterparts, many of us just don't like to bother with what most consider the trickiest part of the pie, its crust!

Pie crusts don't have to be difficult, not anymore. In fact, with some of the newer recipes there's literally nothing to it at all!

By combining a few basic pie principles with a few good recipes, some of which are completely goof-proof, you'll soon find that the hardest thing about homemade pies is selecting what filling to use.

Just follow this simple pie crust primer and you will have a perfect pie crust every time!

PIE CRUST PRINCIPLES

1. Do not over mix dough. For a good and flaky crust, make sure to only coat the fat with flour, not blend it in like cookie dough. Try using a food processor and just pulse dough gently until formed.

2. Keep all fat and liquids cold so they stay separated.

3. Less liquid is better than more, and cold is better than warm.

4. When adding liquid don't mix it in. Toss it around so it collects all the flour-coated fat particles together and makes them stick to one another.

5. Poke holes in the top of the pie to vent steam to avoid a mushy pie and a messy oven.

Pies & Cheesecakes

For a good and flaky crust, make sure to only coat the fat with flour, not blend it in like cookie dough. Try using a food processor and just pulse dough gently until formed.

Food That Makes You Feel Good!

Best Butter Pie Crust
3 cups all purpose flour
1 tablespoon granulated sugar
1/2 teaspoon salt
1 cup very cold butter
1 large egg yolk
1 teaspoon vinegar
7 tablespoons water

In a bowl, combine flour with sugar and salt. With a pastry cutter, cut in the butter until the dough is the consistency of tiny peas. In a small bowl, whisk together the egg yolk, vinegar and water. Gently stir egg mixture into the flour mixture until moistened and the dough holds together. Gather into a ball and divide into two pieces. Cover both pieces with plastic wrap and refrigerate for one or more hours. Recipe makes two 9 inch crusts.

(16 servings). Per serving: Calories 180; Fat 8g; Carbohydrates 75g; Protein 10g.

No Roll Pie Crust
A single crust mixes right in the pie plate.
1 1/2 cups all purpose flour
1 teaspoon salt
2 tablespoons granulated sugar
1/2 cup oil
2 tablespoons cold milk

Sift together flour, salt and sugar into pie plate. In a small bowl beat together oil and milk and pour over the flour mixture. Quickly mix with a fork just enough to moisten flour. Press into pie plate, prick all over with a fork and bake at 425 degrees for 15 minutes. Recipe makes one 9 inch pie crust.

Approximate servings per recipe: 8. Per serving: Calories 220; Fat 14g; Carbohydrates 21g; Protein 3g.

Simple Shake Pie Crust
2 1/2 cups all purpose flour
2 tablespoons granulated sugar
1 cup shortening
1/2 cup cold water
1 dash salt

Put flour, sugar, salt and shortening in a plastic bowl with a lid. Seal then shake until it sounds like sand. Add water, seal, and shake until it sounds like a rock. Roll out for your favorite pie or pastry.

Approximate servings per recipe: 8. Per serving: Calories 190; Fat 1g; Sodium 10mg; Carbohydrates 16g; Fiber 0.5g; Sugar 2g; Protein 2g.

Pies & Cheesecakes

Fried Pie Crust
3 cups all purpose flour
1 cup solid trans fat free shortening
1 teaspoon fine sea salt
1 large egg
1/3 cup cold water
1 teaspoon vinegar
filling of your choice
additional shortening for frying

Chill all ingredients. In food processor, pulse flour, 1 cup shortening and salt 5 times then add egg, water, and vinegar and pulse until dough comes clean from sides of bowl. Roll dough out on a floured surface then cut into 3 inch square pieces. Add a tablespoon of filling and pinch dough edges closed to create small triangles. Fry at 350 degrees for 1 to 2 minutes on each side then drain on wire racks.

Approximate servings per recipe: 32. Per serving: Calories 65; Fat 2g; Carbohydrates 3g; Protein 1g. (Nutrition does not include filling.)

Food That Makes You Feel Good!

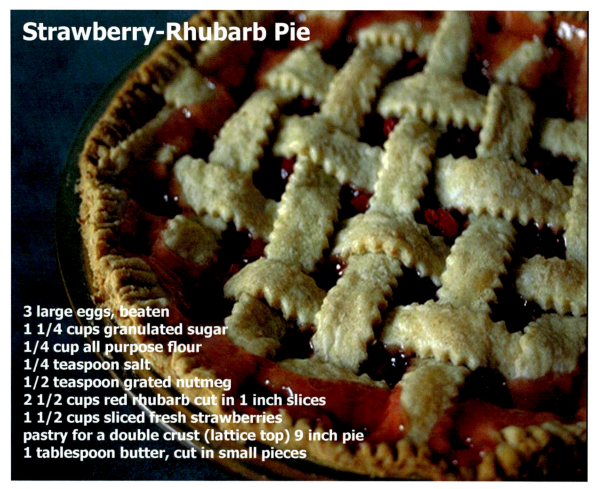

Strawberry-Rhubarb Pie

3 large eggs, beaten
1 1/4 cups granulated sugar
1/4 cup all purpose flour
1/4 teaspoon salt
1/2 teaspoon grated nutmeg
2 1/2 cups red rhubarb cut in 1 inch slices
1 1/2 cups sliced fresh strawberries
pastry for a double crust (lattice top) 9 inch pie
1 tablespoon butter, cut in small pieces

Preheat oven to 425 degrees. Combine eggs, sugar, flour, salt, and nutmeg and mix well. In a separate bowl, combine rhubarb and strawberries. Line 9 inch pie plate with pastry; fill with rhubarb mixture. Pour egg mixture over it and dot with butter. Top with lattice crust and crimp edges high. Bake for 40 minutes. Serve warm, plain or topped with vanilla ice cream.

Approximate servings per recipe: 6. Per serving: Calories 344; Fat 10g; Sodium 304mg; Carbohydrates 59g; Fiber 2g; Sugar 44g; Protein 5g.

Pies & Cheesecakes

I doubt the phrase "Easy as Apple Pie" was coined by a baker, but apple pie doesn't have to be labor-intensive. There are shorcuts that don't cut short taste!

Food That Makes You Feel Good!

Easy Apple Pie
2 refrigerated pie crusts
1 cup granulated sugar
1 tablespoon all purpose flour
1 teaspoon ground cinnamon
5 Granny Smith apples, peeled, cored and sliced
1 yellow apple, peeled, cored and sliced
1 tablespoon butter, cut in small pieces

Preheat oven to 350 degrees. Follow package instructions and fit one pie crust in the bottom of a 9 inch pie plate. In a small bowl combine sugar, flour and cinnamon. Sprinkle flour mixture over apples and stir to coat evenly. Pour apples into pie plate and dot with pieces of butter. Place remaining pie crust on top, crimping edges and making slits in the top crust to allow for steam to escape during baking. Bake pie in the center of the oven for 1 hour. Cover edges with foil if crust becomes too brown.

Approximate servings per recipe: 8. Per serving: Calories 69; Fat 2g; Carbohydrates 14g; Fiber 3g; Protein 1g.

Pies & Cheesecakes

Food That Makes You Feel Good!

Blueberry Pie

2 refrigerated pie crusts
5 cups fresh blueberries
1 tablespoon lemon juice
1 cup granulated sugar
1/3 cup all purpose flour
1/8 teaspoon salt
1/2 teaspoon ground cinnamon
2 tablespoons butter or margarine
1 large egg, lightly beaten
1 teaspoon sugar

Preheat oven to 400 degrees. Sprinkle berries with lemon juice; set aside. Follow package instructions and fit one pie crust in the bottom of a 9 inch pie plate. Combine 1 cup sugar, flour, salt and cinnamon and add to berries, stirring well. Pour into pie shell, and dot with butter. Place remaining crust over filling and crimp edges. Cut slits in top of crust to allow steam to escape. Brush top with beaten egg and sprinkle with 1 teaspoon sugar.
Bake for 35 minutes or until golden.
Cover edges with aluminum foil to prevent over browning, if necessary.
Serve with vanilla ice cream, if desired.

Approximate servings per recipe: 8.
Per serving: Calories 478; Fat 21g; Sodium 410mg; Carbohydrates 69g; Fiber 2g; Sugar 37g; Protein 5g.

Delicious Cherry Pie

1 cup granulated sugar
(1 1/4 cups if using sour cherries)
1/4 cup all purpose flour
1/2 teaspoon cinnamon
4 cups cherries, pitted
pastry for a double crust 9 inch pie
2 tablespoons milk
2 tablespoons sugar for top of pie

Preheat oven to 425 degrees.
In a large plastic bag, combine sugar, flour and cinnamon.
Add cherries then toss to coat.
This coats the cherries more evenly than doing it in a bowl and makes a filling that is firmer.
Place filling in a pastry lined pie pan.
Place remaining crust over filling and crimp edges.
Cut vent slits in top of crust,
brush with milk and sprinkle with sugar.
Bake a for 25 minutes,
reduce heat to 350 degrees
then bake for 25-30 minutes more.

Approximate servings per recipe: 8.
Per serving: Calories 157; Fat 2g; Sodium 39mg; Carbohydrates 40g; Fiber 2g; Sugar 34g; Protein 1g.

Pies & Cheesecakes

Food That Makes You Feel Good!

Kathi's Pear Pie

pastry for a double crust 9 inch pie
1/2 cup dark brown sugar
1/4 cup granulated sugar
pinch of salt
1/4 teaspoon ground ginger
1/4 teaspoon ground cinnamon
2 tablespoons cornstarch
6 pears, peeled, cored and sliced
2 tablespoons fresh lemon juice
1 tablespoon butter, cut into pieces
1 large egg
1 tablespoon heavy cream

Preheat oven to 425 degrees.
In a small bowl, combine sugars, salt, spices and cornstarch. Set aside. Arrange pears slices in the bottom of pie shell.
Sprinkle with sugar mixture then drizzle with lemon juice and dot with butter. Moisten rim of crust with water. Cover with top crust, pinching edges closed and trimming off excess dough. Beat egg and cream together then glaze top of pie with it using a pastry brush. Cut six 2 inch long slits in top of crust. Bake pie in the center of the oven for 1 1/4 hours. Cover edges with foil if crust becomes too brown.

Approximate servings per recipe: 16.
Per serving: Calories 94; Fat 2g;
Carbohydrates 19g; Fiber 2g; Protein 1g.

A pie recipe from 1850 just goes to show how long people have been enjoying God's gift of berries baked into a pie!

1850 Blackberry Pie

2 9 inch unbaked pie crusts
1 quart blackberries
1 cup all purpose flour
2 cups granulated sugar
1 cup milk
1 teapoon of sugar to sprinkle over pie

Preheat oven to 350 degrees. Fill pie shell with berries. In a small bowl, combine flour, sugar and milk. Pour mixture over berries. Cover with top crust, pinching edges closed and trimming off excess dough. Sprinkle sugar over top of pies then bake for 45 to 50 minutes or until center is set.

Approximate servings per recipe: 8.
Per serving: Calories 314; Fat 1g;
Carbohydrates 71g; Fiber 4g; Protein 3.51g.

Pies & Cheesecakes

The Concord grape, a descendant of a plant native to North America, finds its way into everything from jams and jelly to more unique dishes like this pie.

Food That Makes You Feel Good!

Gooey Grape Pie

2 cups green, red or purple grapes, washed, stemmed, seeded
1/4 cup water
1 teaspoon baking soda
1 1/2 cups granulated sugar
1/2 teaspoon ground allspice
1 large egg, beaten
2 tablespoons butter
2 tablespoons Minute tapioca
pastry for a double crust 9 inch pie
1 teaspoon cinnamon
1 tablespoon granulated sugar

Preheat oven to 450 degrees. In a medium saucepan, combine the grapes with water and baking soda. Boil, stirring and mashing as they cook for 5 minutes. Remove from heat and allow to cool. Combine grapes with sugar and allspice then add egg, butter and tapioca. Pour into pie crust and top with remaining crust, sealing edges. Make slits in the top crust for vents. Combine the cinnamon and 1 tablespoon sugar and sprinkle it over the top of the pie. Bake for 10 minutes, then reduce oven to 350 degrees and bake 25 more minutes or until browned. Wrap edges with foil if getting too browned. Cool on wire rack.
Variation: Make with a lattice top.

Approximate servings per recipe: 8.
Per serving: Calories 443; Fat 18g; Carbohydrates 67g; Fiber 2g; Sugar 44g; Protein 4g.

Maple Syrup Pie

1 1/2 cups pure maple syrup
4 large eggs
1/4 teaspoon salt
1 unbaked 9 inch pie crust
1 cup nuts, chopped, toasted (optional)

Preheat oven to 350 degrees. In the bowl of an electric mixer, combine maple syrup, eggs and salt and beat until well combined. Pour mixture into crust, being sure to avoid the edges. Wipe away any spatters or spills on crust edges. Bake pie in the center of the oven for 45 minutes, covering edges with foil if they become too brown.
Top with nuts, if desired.

Approximate servings per recipe: 8.
Per serving: Calories 200; Fat 3g; Carbohydrates 41g; Fiber 0g; Protein 4g.

Pies & Cheesecakes

Food That Makes You Feel Good!

Sweet Potato Pie

2 medium sweet potatoes, washed
1 unbaked 9 inch deep dish pie crust
1/4 cup butter, softened
1 cup dark brown sugar, firmly packed
1 teaspoon ground cinnamon
1/2 teaspoon ground nutmeg
1/4 teaspoon ground cloves
1/4 teaspoon fine sea salt
3 large eggs, slightly beaten
12 ounces evaporated milk
1 cup whipped cream
1/8 teaspoon ground nutmeg

Preheat oven to 450 degrees. Bake sweet potatoes 30 minutes or until tender. Meanwhile, place crust in deep dish pan and line with a double thickness of foil. Bake in same oven for 8 minutes, remove foil and bake for 5 more minutes or until set and dry. Set aside. Reduce oven temperature to 400 degrees. Peel potatoes then place in a large bowl of a mixer and combine with butter, beating until smooth. Beat in sugar, spices and salt. Add eggs, beating on low speed just until combined then slowly stir in evaporated milk. Pour filling into prepared pie shell. Cover edge of pie with foil and bake for 10 minutes. Reduce oven to 350 degrees and bake for 40 to 50 minutes more or until knife inserted in center comes out clean. Cool on wire rack for 1 hour. Serve warm with whipped cream sprinkled with nutmeg.

Approximate servings per recipe: 8.
Per serving: Calories 386; Fat 20g;
Carbohydrates 45g; Fiber 2g; Protein 8g.

Perfect Pumpkin Pie

1 3/4 cups canned pumpkin
1 3/4 cups sweetened condensed milk
2 large eggs, beaten
2/3 cup dark brown sugar, firmly packed
2 tablespoons sugar
1 1/4 teaspoons cinnamon
1/2 teaspoon salt
1 teaspoon ground ginger
1 teaspoon ground nutmeg
1/2 teaspoon ground cloves
9 inch pie shell, unbaked

Preheat oven to 425 degrees. Combine pumpkin and remaining ingredients in a large bowl; beat at medium speed with an electric mixer 2 minutes. Pour into piecrust. Bake at 425 degrees for 15 minutes then reduce oven temperature to 350 degrees and bake 50 additional minutes or until a knife inserted into center of pie comes out clean. Cool on a wire rack.

Approximate servings per recipe: 8.
Per serving: Calories 354; Fat 18g;
Carbohydrates 42g; Fiber 1g;
Sugar 27g; Protein 7g.

Pies & Cheesecakes

Food That Makes You Feel Good!

Icebox pies are named after the old iceboxes that were used to keep food cool in pre-refrigerator days, which didn't become affordable for most people until the late 1940's and early 50's.

Being born in 1961, the only experience I had with an icebox was the one my father had in his motor home.

Before any vacation, Dad would take me to the east side of Chicago to purchase a big block of ice from a gigantic blue vending machine situated in the middle of a liquor store parking lot. He'd grapple with a big, shiny, slick slab; forcefully heaving this bulky block from the machine into the backseat of his Volvo, all the while mumbling how we had to hurry in order to, "Beat the heat!"

Personally, I looked forward to sitting next to the ice. My job was to make sure it didn't slide off the seat, which I'm sure was the real reason he bothered to bring me along.

That big, cool block of crystal sure fascinated me. I couldn't help but run my small fingers across it whenever Dad wasn't looking, so I could feel just how cool it was- real cool!

Once home, Dad would move very quickly to slide the now dripping diamond out of the car and into its spot in the icebox, quickly slamming the door and locking its tiny, clanking clasp in place. Dad would then quickly wipe the sweat from his brow with the bright red handkerchief he always carried in his back pocket and issue the same advice, "If you keep an icebox closed good and tight you can get darn near a whole week of cool out of one block of ice. Remember that. Keep the door closed."

While I never did see any pies come out of Daddy's icebox, as he stocked it solely with fresh caught fish, I was able to find one of the many first icebox pie recipes printed in an old, 1930's Slovak cookbook.

The recipe sounds just as cool and inviting as that block of ice was and nearly just as simple. 'Simply whisk the juice of 3 lemons with 3 raw, (pasteurized) egg yolks then whisk in 1 can of condensed milk and pour into a graham cracker pie crust. Pop the pie in an icebox and in 3 hours it's done!" This recipe will work and you can substitute 8 ounces of cream cheese for the yolks,
if desired.

The icebox may be long gone, but the inkling for an icebox pie will live on forever!

To honor those old iceboxes, here are 3 modern, fruit flavored favorites that are guaranteed to make your tongue feel frosty in a flash! Keep it cool!

Pies & Cheesecakes

Blueberry Icebox Pie
1/4 cup cornstarch
1/4 cup water
5 cups blueberries (fresh or if frozen, thawed), divided use
2/3 cup granulated sugar
1/2 teaspoon cinnamon
1/2 teaspoon nutmeg
1 tablespoon unsalted butter
1 9 inch graham cracker pie crust

In a small bowl, combine cornstarch and water until smooth. In a medium saucepan, combine 3 cups blueberries, sugar, cinnamon, and nutmeg. Stir in cornstarch mixture and cook over medium heat, stirring constantly, until thickened. Cook another 2 minutes, remove from heat and stir in butter and remaining 2 cups of berries. Pour into crust, cover with plastic wrap and chill 6 hours or until set.

Approximate servings per recipe: 6.
Per serving: Calories 279; Fat 8g; Carbohydrates 53g; Fiber 4g; Protein 2g.

NOTE: Be sure to wrap pie very securely or place in an airtight container to keep it from picking up other flavors or odors from inside the refrigerator.

Pineapple Icebox Pie
14 ounces sweetened condensed milk
1/4 cup freshly squeezed lemon juice
16 ounces crushed pineapple, drained
1 cup chopped nuts
8 ounces frozen non-dairy whipped topping, thawed
2 graham cracker pie crusts

In a bowl, combine milk and lemon juice. Stir in pineapple, nuts and whipped topping, mixing well. Pour into crusts and chill well for several hours.

Approximate servings per recipe: 16 (2 pies).
Per serving: Calories 326; Fat 16g; Carbohydrates 40g; Fiber 1g; Protein 6g.

Berried Treasure Pie
1 8 inch graham cracker pie crust
8 ounces cream cheese, softened
1/2 cup granulated sugar
8 ounces non-dairy frozen whipped topping, thawed
1 pound fresh berries

Beat cream cheese and sugar until well blended. Fold in whipped topping. Press into graham cracker crust. Chill at least 3 hours. Slice and serve with berries on top.

Approximate servings per recipe: 16.
Per Serving: Calories 236; Fat 12g; Sodium 137mg; Carbohydrates 29g; Fiber 0.5g; Sugar 16g; Protein 2g.

Food That Makes You Feel Good!

Cherry - Chocolate Chip Icebox Pie

40 chocolate wafers
2 tablespoons granulated sugar
2 tablespoons butter, melted
1 large egg white
cooking spray
4 cups vanilla low fat frozen yogurt
1 cup sweet cherries, pitted and chopped
1/2 cup semisweet chocolate mini chips
1/2 cup black cherry preserves, melted

Preheat oven to 350 degrees. Place cookies in a food processor and process until crumbly. Add sugar, butter and egg white; pulse 5 times or just until moist. Press crumb mixture evenly into a 9 inch pie plate coated with cooking spray.
Bake at 350 degrees for 8 minutes; cool on a wire rack 15 minutes.
Freeze pie crust for 30 minutes.
Meanwhile, place an extra large bowl in freezer. Remove yogurt from freezer and let stand at room temperature while crust is cooling. Spoon yogurt into chilled bowl.
Stir cherries and mini chips into yogurt; freeze 30 minutes or just until set but not solid. Spread preserves over bottom of prepared crust.
Spoon yogurt mixture evenly over preserves. Return to freezer until set.
Cover with plastic wrap and freeze 6 hours or until firm.
Place pie in refrigerator 30 minutes before serving to soften.

Approximate servings per recipe: 9. Per serving: Calories 288; Fat 9g; Carbohydrates 49g; Fiber 1g; Protein 1g.

Pies & Cheesecakes

5 Minute Mini Lemon Pies
1 1/2 cups vanilla yogurt
6 single serving size graham cracker pie crusts
11 ounces prepared lemon curd

GARNISH
grated rind of 1 lemon

Into each pie crust spoon 2 tablespoons of lemon curd. Top with about 1/4 cup of vanilla yogurt, sprinkle with lemon rind and serve or refrigerate.

Approximate servings per recipe: 6: Per Serving: Calories 210; Fat 12g; Sodium 255mg; Carbohydrates 25g; Fiber 1g; Sugar 18g; Protein 10g.

Grasshopper Pie
1 pint mint chocolate chip ice cream
8 ounces frozen non-dairy whipped topping, thawed
1 ounce Cream de Menthe liquor
1 chocolate graham cracker pie crust

Remove ice cream from freezer and let stand at room temperature for 15 minutes.
In the large bowl of an electric mixer, using the whisk attachment, blend ice cream until smooth. Add whipped topping then the liquor. Pour filling into pie crust and freeze until set. Cover with plastic wrap and freeze 6 hours or until firm. Place pie in refrigerator 30 minutes before serving to soften.

Approximate servings per recipe: 8
Per serving: Calories 340; Fat 17g; Carbohydrates 40g; Fiber 1g; Protein 6g.

Luscious Key Lime Pie
4 large egg yolks
14 ounces sweetened condensed milk
1/2 cup freshly squeezed key lime juice
2 teaspoons grated key lime rind
1 9 inch graham cracker pie shell
4 ounces frozen non-dairy whipped topping, thawed

With an electric mixer on high, beat egg yolks until thick, then add the sweetened condensed milk. Turn mixer to low and slowly mix in lime juice and rind. Continue to mix until well blended. Pour into pie shell and bake at 325 degrees for 30 minutes. Top with whipped topping just before serving.

Approximate servings per recipe: 8.
Per serving: Calories 145; Fat 8g; Carbohydrates 20g; Protein 4g.

Food That Makes You Feel Good!

Best Banana Cream Pie
3/4 cup granulated sugar
1/3 cup all purpose flour
1/4 teaspoon salt
2 cups milk
3 large egg yolks, lightly beaten
2 tablespoons butter
1 teaspoon pure vanilla extract
3 medium firm bananas
1 baked 9 inch pie shell

GARNISH
frozen non-dairy topping, thawed
banana slices

In a saucepan, combine sugar, flour and salt; stir in milk and mix well. Cook over medium heat, stirring constantly, until the mixture thickens and comes to a boil; boil for 2 minutes. Remove from the heat. Stir a small amount of milk mixture into egg yolks, gradually adding enough to bring yolks up in temperature to milk mixture. Transfer this mixture back into saucepan, return to heat and cook for 2 minutes, stirring constantly. Remove from heat, add butter and vanilla, mix well and allow to cool slightly. Slice bananas and place evenly in pie shell. Pour mixture over bananas. Refrigerate for at least 2 hours before serving. Garnish with whipped cream and banana slices, if desired and refrigerate any leftovers.

Approximate servings per recipe: 6.
Per serving: Calories 395; Fat 16g;
Sodium 304mg; Carbohydrates 59g;
Fiber 2g; Sugar 33g; Protein 6g.

Incredible Coconut Pie
1/3 cup all purpose flour
2/3 cup granulated sugar
2 cups milk
2 large egg yolks
1 cup unsweetened flaked coconut
1 teaspoon pure vanilla extract
1 teaspoon butter
1 prepared pie crust
1 aerosol can whipped topping

In medium saucepan mix flour, sugar, milk and egg yolks. Cook and stir until mixture comes to a boil. Boil for 1 minute. Remove from heat and add coconut, vanilla and butter. Pour into crust. Cover with plastic wrap and refrigerate for 3 hours.
Top with whipped toppping.

Approximate servings per recipe: 8.
Per serving: Calories 414; Fat 25g;
Sodium 163mg; Carbohydrates 43g;
Fiber 3g; Sugar 24g; Protein 6g.

Pies & Cheesecakes

Say Cheese!

Ahhh...the pleasure of cheesecake just got even better. "How?" you ask. By the addition of some super rich, incredibly creamy ricotta cheese!

Ricotta, pronounced "ri-kote-a," is an Italian whey cheese, meaning it's usually made from the whey that remains after making whole milk cheese, though it can also be made from whole milk.

In its basic form, ricotta is fresh, creamy, slightly sweet and low fat, typically, around 5% fat, with a finely grained texture and a pure white color. It is somewhat similar in texture to cottage cheese, although it is considerably lighter.

The name ricotta means "cooked again" or "re-cooked" in Italian, referring to the second processing of the liquid done to produce the cheese.

In Italian households and dining establishments, ricotta is often beaten smooth and mixed with condiments, such as sugar, cinnamon and occasionally chocolate shavings, and served in desserts such as cannoli.

In addition to its fresh, soft form, ricotta is also sold in three preparations, which ensure a longer shelf life: salted, baked and smoked.

The pressed, salted and dried variety of the cheese is known as ricotta salata.
A milky-white hard cheese used for grating or shaving, ricotta salata is sold in wheels, decorated by a delicate basket-weave pattern.

Ricotta infornata is produced by placing a large lump of soft ricotta in the oven until it develops a brown, lightly charred crust, sometimes even until it becomes sandy brown all the way through.

Ricotta infornata is popular primarily in Sardinia and Sicily and is sometimes called ricotta al forno.

Ricotta affumicata is similar to ricotta infornata and is produced by placing a lump of soft ricotta in a smoker until it develops a grey crust and acquires a charred wood scent, usually of oak or chestnut wood.

A process - Ricotta scanta - is actually letting ricotta go 'bad' in a controlled manner. It is produced by letting it go sour for about a week, then stirring it every 2-3 days, salting occasionally and allowing the liquid to flow away. After about 100 days, the ricotta becomes like the consistency of cream cheese, with a distinct pungent, piquant aroma, much like blue cheese, but much richer.

Ricotta scanta tastes as it smells, extremely aromatic, piquant and with a definite bitter note. If tasted with the tip of your tongue, it is said to taste hot.

Good ricotta cheese should be firm, not solid and consist of a mass of fine, moist, delicate grains.

To bring out the best of its flavor, try pairing ricotta with almonds, chocolate, cinnamon, cloves, garlic, lemon, nutmeg, nuts, pepper, pine nuts, spinach, sugar, tomatoes and vanilla.

Ricotta's creamy texture and mild flavor make it ideal for desserts and main dishes as well. Here are some remarkable ricotta recipes you are sure to enjoy.

Pies & Cheesecakes

Food That Makes You Feel Good!

You might wonder why you would ever want to make ricotta cheese when you can simply buy a carton at the supermarket, but making fresh ricotta is easier, tastier and more economical than you think and, all you need are three everyday ingredients and about an hour.

The homemade version is simply the best you'll ever taste in this world - silky and creamy, milky and slightly sweet, moist and never grainy. Now, who can say "No" to that?

If you've never made ricotta at home, try it. The cheese is delicious eaten by the spoonful and once you've had your fill of it unadorned, you can turn it into an array of dishes that are as healthful as they are delectable. Just be sure to make plenty.

Here's a simple recipe that will have you richly rewarded with ricotta in no time!

Ricotta cheese from scratch
1 quart whole milk
2 tablespoons freshly squeezed lemon juice

In a heavy saucepan over low heat, bring milk to the scalding point - 150 degrees. Remove from heat, stir in lemon juice and milk should curdle. Let the mixture sit without refrigeration for 2 to 12 hours. This is the mellowing process. The more patient you are, the mellower your cheese will be. Line a strainer with 2 layers of cheesecloth. Place strainer over a bowl and pour the milk mixture into the strainer, allowing the whey to drain several hours until the curd is dry. Flavor as you choose with blue cheese, peanut butter, honey, nuts, fresh or dried herbs, spices or just eat it plain.

Approximate servings per recipe: 4 (1/2cup) portions. Per serving: Calories 158; Fat 9g; Sodium 120 mg; Carbohydrates 12g; Fiber 0g; Sugar 0g; Protein 8g.

Pies & Cheesecakes

Rich Ricotta Cheesecake

CRUST
1 1/2 cups chocolate wafer crumbs
2 tablespoons granulated sugar
1/4 cup butter, melted

FILLING
4 cups (2 pounds) ricotta cheese
1 cup granulated sugar
1 teaspoon grated lemon rind
2 teaspoons pure vanilla extract
1/4 teaspoon salt
4 large eggs
cooking spray
1 tablespoon powdered sugar

SAUCE
1/2 cup sugar
1/4 cup water
1 teaspoon freshly squeezed lemon juice
pinch of salt
1 cup heavy cream
1 cup brown sugar
1 1/2 cups Granny Smith apples, cored and chopped
1 teaspoon pure vanilla extract

CRUST: Preheat oven to 350 degrees. In a small bowl, combine wafer crumbs, sugar and melted butter. Press into the bottom and 1 1/2 inches up the sides of a greased 9 or 10 inch spring form pan. Bake at 350 for 10 minutes. Cool on a wire rack.

FILLING: In a large bowl combine ricotta, sugar, lemon rind, vanilla extract and salt. Beat with a mixer at medium speed 2 minutes or until smooth. Add eggs, 1 at a time, beating well after each addition. Pour batter into a 9 or 10 inch spring form pan coated with cooking spray. Bake for 1 hour or until cheesecake center barely moves when pan is touched. Remove cheesecake from oven and run a knife around the outside edge of cheesecake. Cool slightly then remove outer ring from pan. Sprinkle cheesecake evenly with powdered sugar.

SAUCE: In a heavy saucepan, bring water, sugar, lemon juice and salt to a boil. Cover pan and let boil for 3 minutes. Uncover and boil until mixture turns the color of iced tea, 5 to 6 minutes. Whisk in cream and brown sugar. Reduce heat to low and simmer for 2 minutes. Cool to room temperature. Just before serving stir apples and vanilla into cooled sauce and spoon over cheesecake.

Approximate servings per recipe: 12.
Per serving: Calories 286; Fat 10g; Sodium 328 mg; Carbohydrates 32g; Fiber 3g; Protein 18g.

Food That Makes You Feel Good!

Chocolate Truffle Cheesecake

CRUST
1 1/2 cups chocolate wafer crumbs
2 tablespoons granulated sugar
1/4 cup butter, melted

FILLING
1/4 cup semisweet chocolate chips
1/4 cup heavy whipping cream
24 ounces cream cheese, softened
1 cup granulated sugar
1/3 cup baking cocoa powder
3 large eggs
1 teaspoon pure vanilla extract

TOPPING
1 1/2 cups semisweet chocolate chips
1/4 cup heavy whipping cream
1 teaspoon pure vanilla extract

GARNISH
1 aerosol can whipped topping
miniature milk chocolate candy kisses

CRUST: Preheat oven to 350 degrees. In a small bowl, combine wafer crumbs, sugar and melted butter. Press into the bottom and 1 1/2 inches up the sides of a greased 9 inch spring form pan. Bake at 350 for 10 minutes. Cool on a wire rack. Reduce oven heat to 325 degrees.
FILLING: In a saucepan over low heat, melt 1/4 cup chocolate chips, stirring until smooth. Remove from heat, add 1/4 cup heavy whipping cream and mix well. Set aside. In a mixing bowl, beat cream cheese and 1 cup sugar until smooth. Add cocoa and beat well. Add eggs, beating on low just until combined. Stir in 1 teaspoon vanilla and reserved chocolate mixture just until blended. Pour over crust. Bake for 45 to 50 minutes or until center is almost set.
TOPPING: Melt 1 1/2 cups chocolate chips in a saucepan over low heat, stirring until smooth. Remove from heat, stir in 1/4 cup heavy cream and 1 teaspoon vanilla. Mix well. Spread over filling. Refrigerate overnight.
Carefully run a knife around the edge of the pan to loosen. Remove the sides of the pan.
GARNISH: Top with whipped cream and miniature chocolate kisses, if desired.

Approximate servings per recipe: 12. Per serving: Calories 542; Fat 38g; Carbohydrate 47g; Fiber 3g; Protein 9g.

Pies & Cheesecakes

Superb New York Style Cheesecake

CRUST
2 cups ground graham cracker crumbs
2 tablespoons granulated sugar
1/2 cup butter, melted

FILLING
40 ounces cream cheese, softened
1 3/4 cups granulated sugar
2 tablespoons all purpose flour
1 1/2 teaspoons pure vanilla extract
5 large eggs
2 large egg yolks
1/3 cup whipping cream
1 teaspoon finely grated lemon rin

GARNISH
Fresh Berries

Preheat oven to 325 degrees.
CRUST: Combine graham cracker crumbs and melted butter. Stir until well combined. Press onto bottom and about 2-1/2 inches up the sides of a 9x3 inch spring form pan.
FILLING: Mix cream cheese, sugar, flour, and vanilla. Beat with an electric mixer until fluffy. Add eggs and egg yolks, beating on low speed just until combined. Stir in whipping cream and lemon rind. Pour into prepared crust. Place pan in the oven and bake about 1 1/2 hours or until center appears nearly set when shaken. Cool 15 minutes. Loosen crust from sides of pan. Cool 30 minutes more; remove sides of pan. Cool completely. Chill 4 to 24 hours.
GARNISH: If desired, garnish with fresh berries.

Approximate servings per recipe: 12. Per serving: Calories 637; Fat 47g; Sodium 451mg; Carbohydrates 44g; Fiber 0.4g; Sugars 33.9g; Protein 11g.

Food That Makes You Feel Good!

Sugar-Free New York Style Cheesecake

**24 packets sugar substitute
2 large egg whites
2 large eggs
2 tablespoons cornstarch
1 tablespoon fresh lemon juice
24 ounces cream cheese, softened
1 cup sour cream
1 teaspoon pure vanilla extract**

Preheat oven to 300 degrees. In a bowl, beat cheese and sugar substitute until fluffy. Beat in egg whites, then eggs and cornstarch. Beat in vanilla, lemon juice and sour cream. Pour mixture into a greased spring form pan. Bake for 60 minutes. Turn off oven and let cake sit in oven until completely cooled. Refrigerate overnight. Serve the next day.

Calories 260; Fat 25g; Protein 7g; Carbohydrates 4g.

Pies & Cheesecakes

The best recipes are the ones that are the most versatile. Take this no nonsense, No Bake Cheesecake Pie. With the help of different toppings, you can turn this dandy little recipe into a number of delectable delights!

Food That Makes You Feel Good!

No Bake Cheesecake Pie
8 ounces cream cheese, softened
1/2 cup granulated sugar
1 tablespoon freshly squeezed lemon juice
8 ounces frozen non-dairy whipped topping, thawed
1 prepared graham cracker crust

In a mixer, blend cream cheese, sugar and lemon juice, and then fold in whipped topping. Pour into graham cracker crust, spreading cream cheese mixture evenly against sides. Chill at least 3 hours before serving. Just before serving, top with whatever you like, berries being preferable.

Approximate servings per recipe: 8. Per serving: Calories 473; Fat 25g; Carbohydrate 59g; Fiber 1g; Sugars 31g; Protein 4g.

Special Desserts

Food That Makes You Feel Good!

Henry David Thoreau once wrote, "It is remarkable how closely the history of the apple tree is connected with that of man."

What Thoreau was referring to was that like man, each apple holds seeds with the potential for future life and like man, each seed contains information to produce a completely new and different tree that, if planted and grown, will only bear a slight resemblance to its parents.

Each apple tree is as unique and different as each human being that comes into this world. Amazing, isn't it?

The fact that apples don't come "true" from seed creates a production problem for varieties that are adored, like Golden Delicious. In order to produce more Golden Delicious apples, a branch needs to be removed from the mother tree and grafted onto new rootstock, thus creating a clone. What this means then is every apple bearing the name Golden Delicious is in fact, a clone of the original Golden Delicious apple tree that first grew in West Virginia way back in the late 1800's - truly amazing!

It makes me wonder if Thoreau ever gave any thought to man eventually trying to graft/clone everything he adored?

In apple lore there is perhaps no greater tale than that of John Chapman, a.k.a. Johnny Appleseed, who was known for planting apple seeds all over the Ohio area. However, all of Johnny's apples came from seeds, making them spitters, which are good for only two things - vinegar and hard cider.

When you consider this, it's likely that Johnny's true popularity did not come from providing food as people think, but rather for providing an alcohol source for the new frontier.

Likewise, Carry Nation's hatchet - the symbol of Prohibition - was more likely not to symbolize the chopping down of saloon doors as is thought, but rather the chopping down of all those hard cider producing apples trees Johnny Appleseed planted so prolifically.

What's ironic is if it were not for the quick thinking of the apple (cider) growers of the time, who came up with the brilliant slogan, "An apple a day keeps the doctor away," all the apple trees in America might have been felled for the sake of Prohibition.

Apples are good for you. They cleanse the teeth and they strengthen the gums while you eat them.

They lower cholesterol levels and they bind with toxins in the body -especially heavy metals - and shuttle them out. They also help destroy viruses, neutralize indigestion, prevent constipation, relieve gout and rheumatism and are very soothing and antiseptic.

Apples are so good for you that instead of one a day, you should eat two! Here are some of my favorite apple recipes, including an heirloom, Apple Slices recipe that is a treasured one from my mother's private collection.

103

Special Desserts

Food That Makes You Feel Good!

Taffy Apple Salad

8 ounces crushed pineapple in juice
1 tablespoon all purpose flour
1/4 cup granulated sugar
1 large egg
2 tablespoons apple cider vinegar
8 ounces non-dairy whipped topping, thawed
1 1/2 cups Spanish peanuts
4 eating apples, washed, skins on
GARNISH: Melted caramel, optional

Drain pineapple and save juice. In a small saucepan combine flour and sugar and blend well. In a cup, beat egg, vinegar and pineapple juice. Slowly add egg mixture into sugar mixture, stirring well. Heat on low, stirring till thickened. Cool then combine with pineapple, whipped topping, and peanuts. Core then chop apples directly into mixture. Refrigerate for 2 hours before serving.

Approximate servings per recipe: 8. Per serving: Calories 315; Fat 18g; Carbohydrates 29g; Fiber 4g; Sugar 24g; Protein 10g.

Easy Applesauce

1/2 cup water
4 Granny Smith apples
1/4 cup granulated sugar
1/2 teaspoon cinnamon
1/4 teaspoon ground cloves
1/4 teaspoon pure vanilla extract
1/2 teaspoon fresh lemon juice

Peel, core and quarter apples. Place in a heavy saucepan with a tightly fitting lid. Add remaining ingredients, bring to a boil, cover, and simmer until apples break down, about 20 minutes. Continue to simmer until sauce reaches desired consistency.

Approximate servings per recipe: 2. Per serving: Calories 241; Fat 0.5g; Sodium 4 mg; Carbohydrates 63g; Fiber 7g; Protein 1g.

Special Desserts

An Apple a day...

Offering plenty of cleansing fiber and many tasty varieties, it only makes sense to include more apples in your life!

Food That Makes You Feel Good!

Millennium Apples 101

The only apple adage I can ever quickly recall is, "Spies for pies," meaning Northern Spy apples are best for baking.

These apples, like Granny Smith are the baking apples of choice because they don't turn into runny applesauce when heated.

Nowadays, Michigan is growing more new apple varieties than any other state, including Washington - apples we cooks and cookbooks know nothing about, making a little "Apples 101" quite useful.

Here's a cheat sheet to help figure out what's best on today's apple carts!

Empire: A long keeper with a McIntosh mild tartness and a Red Delicious sweetness. Great for any use.

Jonagold: An all-purpose apple, great for any use, with flavors ranging from sweet to tart, and ranked the world's best apple.

Ginger Gold: Firm and white-fleshed, with a spicy-sweet flavor. Best for eating out of hand and in salads.

Redcort: Very red. Good for eating out of hand and for sauces and ciders.

Gala: An early apple with an especially fine eating quality - sweet, zesty flesh in a gold or red-blushed package. Rated second best in the world.

Fuji: Superb eating and dessert apple. It's crisp, juicy, and fragrant, with low acid and sweet flavor. Fuji keeps longer than most at room temperature.

Braeburn: Crisp, firm and juicy. Late-season, long storage life, good for cooking and eating.

Spartan: Firmer and crisper than the McIntosh, with rich flavor and excellent juiciness. A fragrant apple, good for cooking and eating, and cider.

Honey Gold: The flesh is crisp, yellow, juicy, and has a flavor similar to Golden Delicious.

Macoun: Extra sweet, aromatic and juicy with a hint of crunch. Macouns are known as a perfect apple with cheese and wine and are also great for salads and sauce.

Honey Crisp: Crossed with Macoun and the Honeygold, this apple is considered an "extra fancy" sweet and juicy eating apple.

Today's apples are more versatile. Here are some recipes that prove just that!

Special Desserts

Caramel Apple Strudel
6 cups Granny Smith apples, sliced
3/4 cup dark brown sugar
2 teaspoons cinnamon
8 ounces phyllo pastry, 1/2 box, thawed
1 cup butter, melted
1 bag of caramels, melted
1/4 cup chopped nuts, optional

Preheat oven to 400 degrees. Mix apples with sugar and cinnamon and set aside.
Place 1 phyllo sheet on a kitchen towel and sprinkle with melted butter. Place a second sheet on top of it and sprinkle with butter again. Repeat until 6 -8 leaves have been used. Mound 1/2 of the apple mixture in a 3-inch strip along the narrow end of the phyllo, leaving a 2-inch border. Lift towel, using it to roll dough over apples, jelly roll fashion. Brush top of the strudel with butter and sprinkle with cinnamon, if desired. Repeat the entire procedure for the second strudel. Bake the strudels for 20 to 25 minutes or until browned. Drizzle with melted caramel and sprinkle with nuts, if using.

Approximate servings per recipe: 16 Per serving: Calories 474; Fat 27g; Sodium 457 mg; Carbohydrates 53g; Fiber 4g; Sugar 19g; Protein 7g.

VARIATION: Omit caramel and nuts and top with this sauce instead.

Sublime Sauce
1/2 cup heavy whipping cream
1/2 cup sour cream
1/4 teaspoon pure vanilla extract
1/8 teaspoon salt
3 tablespoons powdered sugar

Mix sour cream and heavy cream well and let stand at room temperature for 1 hour or until thickened like yogurt. Just before serving stir in remaining ingredients. Pour over strudel slices.

Food That Makes You Feel Good!

Mom's Marvelous Apple Slices

FILLING
3 pounds cooking apples, peeled, cored, cut into 1/8ths
1 cup water
1 1/4 cup granulated sugar
1 1/2 teaspoons cinnamon
1/4 teaspoon salt
2 tablespoons cornstarch
1/4 cup cold water

In a 2 quart saucepan, bring water, sugar, cinnamon and salt to a boil. Add apples and simmer for ten minutes. Blend cornstarch in 1/4 cup cold water. Stir into hot mixture. Simmer for 5 minutes, stirring gently. Cool before using.

CRUST
2 cups all purpose flour
1/2 teaspoon baking powder
1/2 teaspoon salt
3/4 cup vegetable shortening
2 large egg yolks, beaten
1 teaspoon freshly squeezed lemon juice
1/4 cup water

In a large mixing bowl, combine flour, baking powder and salt. Cut shortening into flour until it resembles peas. In a cup, mix egg yolks, lemon juice and water. Slowly sprinkle egg mixture over flour mixture and blend in lightly until dough is easy to handle. Divide dough in half, then roll out one piece for the bottom of a 13-inch by 9-inch pan.

Fill with cooled apple mixture. Roll out remaining dough to fit the top and seal edges. Cut steam vents in top. Bake at 450 degrees for 20 minutes. Reduce oven temperature to 350 degrees and bake for an additional 30 minutes. Let cool for 20 minutes then frost with icing.

ICING
1/3 cup butter
2 cups powdered sugar
1-1/2 teaspoons pure vanilla extract
2 to 4 tablespoons hot water

In a small saucepan melt butter, then add powdered sugar and vanilla. Bring to a boil. Add water 1 tablespoon at a time till you reach desired consistency.
Remove from heat and very quickly drizzle top of apple slices with icing. If icing starts to set, return to heat to soften.

Approximate servings per recipe: 24. Per serving: Calories 247; Fat 9g; Carbohydrates 39g; Fiber 1g; Sugar 30g; Protein 1g.

Special Desserts

Perk up with Pears!

Food That Makes You Feel Good!

The Greek poet Homer loved pears so much that he called them the "gift of the gods." The Romans liked them so much so that they used grafting techniques to develop more than fifty different varieties!

In natural medicine pears are used as a diuretic and laxative. Rich in pectin and soluble fiber, pears can help lower harmful cholesterol levels and, eating pears regularly is said to give you a clear, healthy complexion and glossy, shiny hair. Pears are also low in carbohydrates and a good source of B-complex vitamins and vitamin C and trace amounts of phosphorus and iodine.

Here are some pleasing ways to make the most of a pear's appeal. Enjoy!

Pear Parfaits
3 tablespoons butter
4 tablespoons granulated cane sugar
3 large pears, peeled, cored, and sliced into 1/4" pieces
4 sprigs of fresh rosemary
1 Crème Fraiche recipe (on right)

Melt butter in small skillet. Add sugar and cook at medium heat until caramelized. Add sliced pears and rosemary sprigs. Cook for 5 minutes. Remove rosemary sprigs and discard. Cool pears. Layer pears alternately with crème fraiche in dessert glasses before serving.

Approximate servings per recipe: 4. Per serving: Calories 168; Fat 2g; Carbohydrates 12g; Protein 1g.

Super-simple Creme Fraiche
2 tablespoons brown sugar
1 dash salt
1 cup sour cream
1/2 cup whipping cream

Sprinkle sugar and salt over sour cream. Let stand 2 minutes. Fold in whipping cream. Refrigerate at least 1 hour before using.

Approximate servings per recipe: 4. Per serving: Calories 168; Fat 13g; Carbohydrates 10g; Protein 2g.

A pear parfait is the perfect end to any meal!

Special Desserts

Spiced Pears

2 cups water
1 cup honey
1 cup cider vinegar
2 cinnamon sticks
2 teaspoons whole cloves
10 Bartlett pears

Combine all ingredients except pears in a large stainless steal or enameled pot. Bring to boil, reduce heat and simmer for 5 minutes, stirring occasionally. Peel pears and slice in half lengthwise, leaving stem attached to one half. Remove core with a sharp paring knife. Gently place pears in the pot of warm liquid. Cover and poach for 30 minutes. If pears rise above liquid, gently stir them back down to evenly flavor. When tender, allow to cool in the liquid. Place pears, with their liquid, cloves and cinnamon sticks into 3 well washed quart jars. Cover and refrigerate. Allow to stand a few days before serving.
Makes 3 quarts.

Approximate servings per recipe: 36. Per serving: Calories 64; Fat 0g; Carbohydrates 17g; Fiber 2g; Protein 0.25g.

A great hostess gift!

Food That Makes You Feel Good!

Frosted Grapes
2 pounds seedless grapes
2 pasteurized egg whites, beaten
1 (3 ounce) package flavored gelatin

Brush grapes with pasteurized egg whites. Sprinkle with gelatin then dry on a rack.

Approximate servings per recipe: 6. Per serving: Calories 161; Fat 0.25g; Carbohydrates 40g; Fiber 1g; Sugar 36g; Protein 3g.

Frosted grapes make elegant, edible table decorations, super salad toppers or beautiful beverage garnishes. For extra flavor try using lime flavored gelatin on green grapes or grape flavored gelatin on blue or red grapes.

Special Desserts

Food That Makes You Feel Good!

Have you ever had visions of sugarplums dance in your head? Even if you did, you probably didn't know you were, especially since most of us have no idea what a sugarplum really is, let alone if it can dance.

If you look for sugarplums in old cookbooks you'll find recipes for fruit-filled confections. If you look on the internet, you'll find a tiring list of companies all named "Sugar Plum." If you tough it out, you'll eventually find recipes for cookies made with fruits and nuts.

If you walk away from that computer, go outside and head south you'll eventually find - depending on your location - that sugarplum is a term that denotes a fondness or affection for something or someone, but not food. However, if you walk wayward into the west you'll find a sugar plum that is a fruit the size of an oversized grape.

It tastes as sweet as candy, but this little sweetie is better than any candy you will ever eat because it's packed with antioxidants, potassium, magnesium, iron and vitamin A. Problem is, these little sugar plums are only available at the end of summer.

If you don't grab them then you'll have to settle for prunes. Yes, prunes, which have become nature's top ranked source of cancer and disease fighting antioxidants.

Prunes also scored number 1 in the ORAC (Oxygen Radical Absorbance Capacity) test, which measures antioxidant power.

Prunes are high in fiber, reduce the risk of colorectal cancer, help prevent as well as treat cardiovascular disease, breast cancer, diabetes and diverticular disease.

All plums and prunes are good for you and all are good for cooking too!
Look for plums with good color and a full, smooth, relatively heavy feel. They should yield to gentle pressure, especially at the end opposite the stem.

Good quality ripe plums should have a "plumy" smell. Avoid shriveled skin, bruises, brown spots, or ones that feel real hard or excessively soft.

Ripen plums at room temperature out of direct sunlight or in a loosely closed brown paper bag. Ripe plums should be refrigerated and eaten as soon as possible.
Here are some great ways to partake in the pleasures of all things plum - enjoy!

Special Desserts

I never thought I'd like plum soup until I tried it - Fabulous! Especially if you use fresh tarragon. It's like you are eating a super-flavorful slushy or snow cone!

Food That Makes You Feel Good!

Plum-Dandy Cake
8 tablespoons butter, softened, divided use
1/2 cup brown sugar, packed
2 tablespoons water
3 cups pitted sliced plums
1 3/4 cups flour
1/2 cup finely ground pecans
1 cup granulated sugar
1 tablespoon baking powder
1/4 teaspoon salt
1 cup milk
2 large eggs
1 1/2 teaspoons vanilla
1 1/2 teaspoons finely grated orange rind

Preheat oven to 350 degrees. Place 3 tablespoons butter in a 9x9 baking pan. Put in the oven until butter is just melted. Remove from oven and stir in brown sugar and water until combined. Spread into an even layer in the pan. Arrange plum slices on top of the sugar mixture. In a large bowl mix flour, pecans, sugar, baking powder, and salt. Add milk, remaining 5 tablespoons butter, eggs and vanilla. Beat with a mixer on low speed until combined. Beat on medium for 1 minute. Stir in orange rind. Spoon batter over top of plums in pan. Bake for 40-45 minutes, until toothpick inserted in the center comes out clean. Remove from oven and cool on a wire rack for 5 minutes. Loosen sides of cake from pan and invert onto a serving plate. Serve warm.

Approximate servings per recipe: 16:
Per serving: Calories 233; Fat 8g; Sodium 165 mg; Carbohydrates 35g; Fiber 1g; Sugar 22g; Protein 3g.

Pleasingly Plum Soup
1 cup water
1 cup sugar
1/3 cup packed fresh tarragon leaves, chopped.
1/2 honeydew melon, rind removed and flesh chopped
8 large plums, pitted and chopped
juice of 1 lime

In small saucepan, combine sugar, water and tarragon. Bring to a boil, reduce heat and simmer for 15 minutes. Remove pan to freezer for 20 minutes. Place lime juice into a blender. Remove sugar mixture from freezer and carefully strain mixture into blender, discarding tarragon leaves. With blender running, slowly add fruit until pureed. Pour mixture into a freezer bag and chill till slushy. Serve as a cold dessert soup, topped with a sprig of tarragon, if desired.

Approximate servings per recipe: 4.
Per serving: Calories 320; Fat 1g; Sodium 27 mg; Carbohydrates 80g; Fiber 3g; Sugar 73g; Protein 4g.

Special Desserts

Food That Makes You Feel Good!

Cherries have been a part of our history since the beginning of time, most notably as the symbol of virginity.

The best place for cherries is Michigan, where cherries are abundant and cherry pie reigns as the #1 dessert.

Cherries are known medicinally for their tonic-like nature. Considered cleansers and purifiers, cherries are also known for their ability to help arthritis sufferers.

One caveat to both wild and domestic cherries is that their leaves, bark and seeds contain cyanogenic glycosides and as such, chewing of their twigs, eating their seeds or making tea from them can cause poisoning effects, especially to children.

Likewise, all classes of livestock have been killed from eating cherry leaves as they are known to cause difficulty in breathing, spasms, coma, and sudden death.

What's also interesting to note about cherries is that it isn't the sweet cherries that work well in recipes but rather the tart. This is because sweet cherries become bland when they are cooked.

It's those sour, tart cherries that make those fabulous pies, juices, jams, and jellies. Problem is, they aren't available in fresh markets because they are very perishable so, unless you know someone who has a tree nearby you have to buy them canned, frozen or dried.

To use, simply wash, pit and freeze in a single layer on trays lined with paper towels. Once frozen, double-bag in plastic and store in the coldest part of the freezer.

Easy Cherry Tarts

3 cups of fresh or frozen sour cherries
1/2 cup granulated sugar
1 teaspoon fresh lemon juice
1 tablespoon cornstarch
4 puff pastry shells
4 tablespoons whipped cream, optional
Fresh cherries for garnish, optional

In a medium saucepan, bring cherries, sugar, lemon juice and cornstarch to a boil. Simmer for 5 to 10 minutes then set aside to cool. Follow package directions to pre-bake pastry shells. Fill each shell with cherry mixture and top with whipped topping and a cherry if desired.

Approximate servings per recipe: 4:
Per serving: Calories 308; Fat 13g; Sodium 171 mg; Carbohydrates 45g; Fiber 1g; Sugar 26g; Protein 4g.

Special Desserts

Blueberries are berry good!

Blueberries have a remarkable ability to enhance collagen density and strength and provide an anti-inflammatory action, which helps to improve our vascular system.

Food That Makes You Feel Good!

Perhaps the popularity of the color blue is derived from some old primitive instinct lying deep within us, causing us to naturally seek out that which preserves us. When it comes to blueberries, this may be the case because as it turns out, it is the blue in these berries that give it its Samson-like strength for preventing and fighting illness and disease.

The compounds that cause this healing shade of cyan - anthocyanidins and proanthocyanidins - are what give blueberries their remarkable ability to enhance collagen density and strength. They also provide an anti-inflammatory action, making it very helpful in treating rheumatoid and osteoarthritis, varicose veins, hemorrhoids and capillary fragility, and toning overall vascular health.

In Europe, hundreds of tons of blueberries are processed annually for use as an anti-hemorrhagic agent in the treatment of eye diseases, including diabetic retinopathy.

Native to Europe and North America, blueberries have been eaten as a fruit since prehistoric times.

Also known as bilberry and sometimes confused with the tiny huckleberry, ripe fresh berries have a mild laxative effect due to sugar content, while dried berries are very binding, making them very useful in treating diarrhea in children who don't like to take medicine.

Blueberries are also useful for complaints of the gastrointestinal tract, kidneys, and urinary tract, arthritis, gout, and dermatitis and are used externally for treatment of mild inflammation of the mucous membranes of the mouth and throat.

Blueberry leaves have a long history of folk use in treatment of diabetes mellitus.

The anthocyanidin compound myrtillin is what promotes this action. One single dose (1g per day) can produce beneficial effects that last for several weeks.

Blueberry's mild flavor suffocates under heavy flavors. Yogurt's light, cool, tangy texture allows the fruit's sweet, juicy flavors to burst onto your palate, making a very healthy, refreshing and flavorful way to enjoy it.

Special Desserts

My Blue Heaven
1 cup fresh blueberries
1 very ripe nectarine or peach
1 cup plain fat free yogurt
1/2 teaspoon pure vanilla extract

Puree yogurt, 1/2 cup blueberries, and vanilla extract. Arrange sliced nectarine on two plates. Place 1/4 cup of fresh blueberries in the center of each plate; pour 1/2 of the yogurt mixture over each plate; chill till serving.

Approximate servings per recipe: 2. Per serving: Calories 160; Fat 0.5g; Carbohydrates 35g; Protein 5g.

Bluebell Slices

FILLING
10 cups blueberries
2 tablespoons lemon juice
1-1/4 cups sugar
1 teaspoon salt
2 tablespoons cornstarch
1/4 cup water

In a 2-quart saucepan, bring berries, lemon juice, sugar, and salt to a boil and simmer for 7 minutes. In a small cup, blend cornstarch and 1/4 cup of cold water then stir into hot berry mixture. Bring to a boil then remove from heat and place pot in a sink filled with ice water to cool filling down. Stir occasionally.

CRUST
2 cups flour
1/2 teaspoon baking powder
1/2 teaspoon salt
3/4 cup vegetable shortening
1 teaspoon lemon juice
2 egg yolks, beaten
1/4 cup water

ICING
1/3 cup butter
2 cups powdered sugar
1-1/2 teaspoons vanilla extract
2 to 4 tablespoons hot water

In a small saucepan heat butter till melted. Add powdered sugar and vanilla. Bring to a boil. Add water 1 tablespoon at a time till you reach your desired consistency. Remove from heat and very quickly drizzle top of apple slices with icing. If icing starts to set, return to heat to soften up.

In a large mixing bowl, combine flour, baking powder and salt. Cut shortening into flour until mix resembles small peas. In a cup, mix egg yolks, lemon juice and water. Slowly sprinkle egg mixture over flour mixture and blend in lightly till all is incorporated and dough is easy to handle. Use more or less water as needed. Cut dough in half, rolling one piece out for the bottom of a 13-inch by 9-inch pan. Fill with blueberry mixture. Roll out rest of dough to fit the top and seal edges. Cut steam vents into top. Bake at 450 degrees for 20 minutes then reduce temperature to 350 degrees and bake for an additional 30 minutes. Drizzle with icing.

Approximate servings per recipe: 24. Per serving: Calories 247; Fat 9g; Carbohydrates 39g; Fiber 1g; Sugar 30g; Protein 1g.

Special Desserts

Food That Makes You Feel Good!

Birds and bunnies will go to just about any length to grab a meal in a raspberry patch. Even going so far as to get themselves all tangled up in the brutally thorny brambles that quite possibly, could have them meet an untimely death.

What could possibly posses these raspberry-robbing rascals to risk life and limb just to reach this tiny little ruby red treat? Could it be that they know something we don't? Perhaps they do.

We are only just beginning to unravel the secrets that nature has known all along. We've just recently learned that raspberries contain anthocyans, antioxidants that improve vision, help control diabetes, improve circulation, prevent cancer, and retard the effects of aging, particularly memory loss and motor skills.

Raspberries also contain cathechins, which are flavonols that support the antioxidant defense system, contributing to cancer prevention, and quercetin, an anti-carcinogen and antioxidant that is shown to reduce the release of histamine, making it effective against allergies.

Raspberry seeds contain ellagic acid, an awesome scavenger that binds cancer-causing chemicals, making them inactive. It can inhibit the ability of other chemicals, block mutations in bacteria and also prevent the binding of carcinogens to DNA.

Raspberries also naturally contain salicylic acid, a close cousin of aspirin (salicylic acid acetate) which is thought to provide the same protective effect against heart disease.

The leaves of a raspberry are pretty remarkable too. They have been taken for centuries, often as a tea, to hasten childbirth.

The leaves also make a great astringent, externally used as eyewash for conjuctivitis, a mouthwash for mouth and gum problems, and as a lotion for ulcers or wounds.

Maybe God's little creatures have known all along that eating these berries will put a spring in your step and have you singing a happy tune!

Raspberry Refresher
1 cup fresh Raspberries
1 cup frozen Yogurt,
Vanilla or Raspberry
1 Banana
1 tablespoon Raspberry liqueur,
(Optional)

GARNISH
1 sprig of mint

In a blender, blend all ingredients until smooth. Pour into two tall glasses. Garnish with a sprig of fresh mint, if desired.

Approximate servings per recipe: 2.
Per serrving: Calories 140; Fat 0.5 g; Carbohydrates 28g; Fiber 1g; Protein 4g.

Special Desserts

Super Sorbet

Ice is nice, but sorbets are sweeter!

The summer heat can send us all searching for something cool, and what could be more deliciously chilling than a sorbet?

Pronounced "sor-BAY," which is French for sherbet, this dish differs greatly from American sherbet in that it does not contain milk or cream.

Being dairy free, fat free and cholesterol free, sorbets offer a cool way to satisfy the need for something sweet without weighing you down.

Consisting primarily of fruit, sugar and water, sorbets are light enough to eat as a palate cleanser between courses as well as an after meal dessert.

At its simplest, making sorbet involves nothing more than pureeing fruit, adding sugar, water and flavor enhancers then freezing, which in today's new ice cream machines makes it, well, a piece of cake!

Sorbet does require some care to balance all its elements.

Because the character of sorbet depends upon its fruit, freshness and ripeness are key. The riper the fruit, the fuller the flavor and the more natural sugar it will contain.

Sugar is added to sorbet not only to increase its sweetness, but also to give it a smoother texture. It does this by lowering its freezing point so it cannot freeze rock hard.

However, the amount of sugar you need to add will depend upon the fruit's fiber content. Too much sugar can result in a soupy sorbet, and too little can make it hard.

A semi-scientific method to determine the proper amount of sugar is to place a whole raw egg, still in its shell, on top of the sorbet mixture before freezing it. If the egg floats so that only a dime-size portion of the shell is protruding above the liquid sorbet, you have the perfect amount of sugar. If the egg sinks lower, add more sugar. If more than a dime size piece of the eggshell is protruding, too much sugar is present. To correct, simply dilute by adding water.

Sorbet is known for its intense flavor. Lemon or lime juice will increase tartness while balancing the sugar so your sorbet is not too sweet.

Alcohol not only adds flavor but, like antifreeze in a car, works with the sugar to lower the freezing point and prevent the sorbet from becoming hard.

Red wine works well with berries, rum goes well with mango. Tequila pairs well with grapefruit or lime and unflavored vodkas can be used to soften sorbet without altering the flavor.

Be sure to use no more that 1 to 2 tablespoons of alcohol per cup of moderately sweet fruit mixture, otherwise you will end up with slush.

Here are some super sorbet selections that are sure to please. Enjoy!

Food That Makes You Feel Good!

Chocolate Sorbet

1 cup cocoa powder
3/4 cup granulated sugar
2 1/2 cups water
1 teaspoon pure vanilla extract

In a heavy saucepan over medium heat, combine cocoa, sugar and water. Bring to a boil. Remove from heat and stir in vanilla. Transfer to a container, cover and refrigerate until chilled. Transfer mixture to ice cream maker and follow manufacturer's instructions. Alternately, place in an 8-inch square pan, cover and freeze, stirring every hour, until desired firmness is attained. Keep in airtight container and frozen until use.

Approximate servings per recipe: 8. Per serving: Calories 98; Fat 1.5g; Carbohydrate 24g; Fiber 3g; Sugars 19g; Protein 2g.

Simple Mango Sorbet

2 1/4 cups peeled ripe mango pieces
1/2 cup unsweetened orange juice
1/4 cup honey

In a blender, combine mango, orange juice and honey and process until smooth. Transfer mixture to an ice cream maker and follow manufacturer's instructions. Alternately, place in an 8-inch square pan, cover and freeze, stirring every hour, until desired firmness is attained. Keep in airtight container and frozen until use.

Approximate servings per recipe: 5. Per serving: Calories 110; Fat 0.3g; Carbohydrate 29g; Fiber 1g; Sugars 27g; Protein 1g

Raspberry Sorbet

12 ounces fresh, slightly chopped raspberries
1 1/2 cups granulated sugar
juice of 1/2 lemon
1 cup cold water
1/4 cup dry red wine, Chambord or cream de cacao
1/4 cup light corn syrup

In a mixing bowl, combine raspberries, sugar and lemon juice and cover. In a separate container, combine liquor, corn syrup and water. Refrigerate both containers for 1 hour. To freeze, add liquor mixture to berry mixture and stir gently until blended.
Transfer mixture to ice cream and follow manufacturer's instructions. Alternately, place in an 8 inch square pan, cover and freeze, stirring every hour, until desired firmness is attained. Keep in airtight container and frozen until use.

Approximate servings per recipe: 6.
Per serving: Calories 272; Fat 1g; Carbohydrate 68g; Fiber 3g; Sugars 56g; Protein 0.7g.

127

Special Desserts

At around 50 calories each, these remarkable Reverse Cheesecakes offer you all the contentment of eating cheesecake without all the fattening consequences.

Food That Makes You Feel Good!

Strawberry Fields Forever

Perhaps the 17th Century English writer Dr. William Butler described the strawberry best when he said, "Doubtless God could have made a better berry, but doubtless God never did."

Originally called strewberries, after the way the berries appear to be strewn about their leaves, the strawberry is indeed unique. Besides being the only fruit with seeds on the outside rather than the inside, its delicate heart-shape has long been a symbol of purity, passion and healing.

Strawberry's European history dates all the way back to the late 13th century, when it was cultivated initially for its medicinal properties. However, American history with this berry's goodness did not begin until around 1835.

Today, the strawberry grows in every state in the United States and every province of Canada, making it the most important small fruit crop grown in the western hemisphere. When selecting strawberries be sure to select ripe berries because strawberries are unable to ripen once plucked from the plant. However, do not buy overripe berries unless you plan to use them immediately. Otherwise, you'll be left with a moldy mess!

Here are some richly rewarding recipes that bring out the very best in these berries. Enjoy!

Reverse Cheesecake
8 ounces Neufchatel cheese, softened
2 teaspoons pure vanilla extract
3 tablespoons powdered sugar or substitute
20 fresh strawberries (1 quart)

GARNISHES (Optional)
Slivered, toasted almonds
Dark chocolate, melted
Powdered sugar

Rinse, drain and dry strawberries well. Remove crown and shave enough off the bottom of the berry so that it will stand up by itself. Arrange berries on a serving dish, crown side up. In a bowl, combine the cheese, vanilla extract and 3 tablespoons powdered sugar and mix well. Fill a cake-decorating bag with large tip with cheese mixture. Pipe the mixture into the tops of the berries, filling them equally. Garnish with toasted almonds, a drizzle of melted dark chocolate or a light dusting of powdered sugar, if desired and chill until serving.

Approximate servings per recipe: 20.
Per serving: Calories 49; Fat 3g; Carbohydrates 3g; Fiber 0.40g; Protein 1g.

Special Desserts

Food That Makes You Feel Good!

Doughnut-dipped Strawberries
The taste of a jelly doughnut without all the fat - I love it!

1 pint fresh strawberries	1 cup graham cracker crumbs
1 cup all purpose flour	1 teaspoon cinnamon
1 large egg	Canola oil for frying
1/2 cup milk	1/2 cup granulated sugar

Wash, stem and pat dry strawberries with paper towels. Put flour in a shallow dish. Blend graham crackers, cinnamon and place in another shallow dish. Beat egg and milk together in a small deep bowl. Dredge strawberries first in the flour then dip in the egg mixture and then press into the cracker mixture. Heat oil in a small deep, heavy pot to 350 degrees. Working with small batches, place strawberries in oil and deep fry for 2 minutes. Drain on paper towels then roll in sugar.

Alternate cooking method: Place 4 berries on a microwave-safe plate, spray berries with cooking spray then microwave at high power for 2 minutes.
NOTE: Tastes even better when dipped in whipped cream!

Approximate servings per recipe: 4. Per fried serving: Calories 290; Fat 6g; Carbohydrates 50g; Fiber 3g; Protein 9g.

Extravagant Strawberries
2 large chocolate candy bars, your favorite brand
12 large fresh strawberries, stems on
Favorite toppings, optional

Leave the stems on your berries. Wash and dry well. Break chocolate into pieces and place in microwave safe bowl. Heat in microwave oven on high for 30 seconds. Stir and if needed, cook for 10 more seconds. Do not over cook as chocolate scorches easily.
Holding by stems, dip each strawberry in to melted chocolate then dip or roll strawberry in your favorite topping, optional and place on wax paper to cool.

Approximate servings per recipe: 6. Per serving: Calories 125; Fat 5g; Carbohydrates 15g; Protein 1g.

Special Desserts

Diamonds may be a girl's best friend, but chocolate is her lover and, with so many men sharing this same passion, there just may be no better way to serve chocolate than from a fountain flowing with it!

Food That Makes You Feel Good!

Do you think it is a coincidence that both Valentine's Day and National Chocolate Fondue Day both land in the same month - February? I think, "Not!"

Yes, there really is a national holiday set aside for us to enjoy one of the most decadent way to get that chocolate freak on - by diving into a huge bowl of it! But, while researching this sweet holiday my eyes melted on a few conflicting facts.

First, fondue is said to be of Swiss origin, made with white wine and melted Emmenthaler or Gruyere cheese. However, the term 'fondue', in fact, is derived from the French word 'fondre', which means 'to melt.' Hmmm....

Then, when it comes to chocolate fondue, it is reported that in the early 1960s, Konrad Egli, a chef at New York's Chalet Suisse Restaurant created this delightful dessert.
However, other articles indicate otherwise.

According to Jane and Michael Stern (American Gourmet, 1991), "Chocolate fondue, unlike cheese fondue, is not Swiss, it was dreamed up in the Madison Avenue test kitchens of the Switzerland Association to promote Toblerone Swiss chocolate."

The Stern's don't say when the great event took place, but they do distinctly remember chocolate fondue being a late-'50s to early '60s phenomenon in their American Century Cookbook (p. 403).

According to other sources, the chocolate fondue has been in existence in one form or another since the 1930's, as is evidenced by a recipe posted in the April 1931, Fitchburg (MA) Sentinel, pg. 10, col. 4:
Chocolate fondue - Add 1-3 cup sugar and 2 squares chocolate, melted over hot water, just after the eggs yolks are added.

We may never know for sure, but just knowing it has been in existence for so long gives me a sweet sense of comfort.

Knowing that this uber decadent way of imbibing in chocolate was around for our ancestors fills me with the hope that perhaps even my grandmother had a chance to enjoy this treat at least once in her short life.

In honor of National Chocolate Fondue Day, Valentines Day and for that matter, any old day chocolate sounds good, here is a sweet,sweet, sweet selection of old and new ways to keep chocolate flowing any time the mood hits you.

Don't forget! The best dippers for a chocolate fondue are strawberries, bananas, pineapples, grapes, tiny cream puffs and marshmallows. Here's to chocolate!

NOTE: Nutrition was not available for these recipes, which is probably a blessing because we'd rather not know!

Special Desserts

There is nothing more festive or fun to share with family and friends than a fabulous-looking fountain overflowing with your favorite food - Chocolate!

Food That Makes You Feel Good!

Chalet Suisse Chocolate Fondue
9 ounces of chocolate
1/2 cup of heavy or light cream
2 tablespoons Kirsch, optional

In a saucepan, break chocolate into small pieces. Add cream, stirring over a low heat. Cook until the chocolate melts and becomes smooth. Add liquor then pour into a fondue pot. Keep on low heat.

Chocolate Fondue
3/4 cup of heavy cream
12 ounces of semi-sweet chocolate
2 tablespoons corn syrup

In a saucepan, heat the cream without allowing it to boil. Remove from heat and add the chocolate pieces. Let chocolate soften for a few minutes then add corn syrup and whisk well. Pour into a fondue pot, using heating element to keep it warm.

Chocolate Fondue a la Blanc
8 ounces heavy cream
12 ounces white chocolate
1 ounce cherry brandy

In a double boiler, combine cream and chocolate, stirring until chocolate is completely melted, making sure not to overcook. Pour mixture into fondue pot, add brandy. Keep warm over a low heat.

Chocolate Fountain
24 ounces semi-sweet chocolate chips
3 unsweetened chocolate squares, finely chopped
3/4 cup canola oil
1/4 cup Kahlua (optional)

In a large glass bowl, place chocolate and oil. Microwave on medium-high for 2 minutes, stir and then microwave for an additional minute or until smooth. Stir in the Kahlua, if desired. Pour chocolate into the heated base of the fountain. Turn on fountain. If the chocolate does not flow smoothly, add additional oil. Suggested dippers: Strawberries, pineapples, bananas, apple slices, marshmallows, Maraschino cherries, pretzels, cream puffs, cookies, rice cake treats and graham crackers.

Approximate servings per recipe: 20. Per serving: Calories Fat 21g; Carbohydrate 23g; Fiber 3g; Sugars 18g; Protein 2g

Special Desserts

Taming Chocolate's Temper

Don't be fooled by its size. This tempting, tiny torte has a tremendously tantalizing texture that will do more than just please a chocolate lover.

Food That Makes You Feel Good!

Many of us have a true passion for chocolate, but when chocolate is not handled and cooked properly, it can get testy. Here are the five top tips and techniques to help you tame your chocolate's temper!

1. **Keep It Cool!** Chocolate is best kept in a dry, cool place between 60 and 78 degrees. Wrapping chocolate in moisture-proof wrap is wise if the temperature is high or the humidity is above 50 percent. Chocolate can be stored in the fridge; but let it stand at room temperature before using. Cocoa is less sensitive to temperature and humidity and can be stored in a tightly covered container in a cool, dry place and be just fine.

2. **Don't get the blues over the bloom!** If your chocolate has a white, crusty-looking film on it, don't toss it out! This is called "bloom" and develops when the chocolate is exposed to varying temperatures, from hot to cold.
   This change in heat allows the cocoa butter to melt and rise to the surface of the chocolate. It doesn't affect the quality or flavor and the chocolate will look normal again once it's melted or used in baking, so keep it!

3. **Master the melting!** Chocolate needs to be heated carefully as it scorches very easily. Never heat dark chocolate above 120 degrees, white or milk chocolate above 110 degrees. Cutting up the chocolate into bits or shavings before melting reduces heating time too. The best way to melt most types of chocolate is in the microwave uncovered in a microwavable dish or bowl on Medium (50%), stirring once every minute, just until melted.
   Some chocolate retains its shape when softened, so stir frequently.

4. **Keep it dry!** Take care never to let water get in chocolate while it's melting. If this happens, the chocolate will get thick, lumpy and grainy, called, "seizing." It will look ruined. "Seized" chocolate can be saved by stirring in 1 teaspoon vegetable oil or shortening for every ounce of chocolate melted.
   Do not use butter or margarine because they contain water.

5. **Keep it smooth!** Little specks of hardened chocolate can appear when stirring melted chocolate into other ingredients. To keep this from happening, melt the chocolate with the liquid or fat that is also called for in the recipe as long as it contains no water. If you use at least 1 tablespoon of liquid or fat to 2 ounces of chocolate, you will avoid the risk of the chocolate "seizing." Never stir cooled, melted chocolate into ice-cold ingredients because the cocoa butter in the chocolate will harden immediately.

Special Desserts

Tiny Chocolate Tortes
(use ganache recipe that follows)
2 ounces semisweet chocolate
1/2 cup walnut pieces
2 tablespoons all purpose flour
3 tablespoons unsalted butter
1/4 cup granulated sugar
2 large eggs, separated
1/2 teaspoon pure vanilla extract
pinch of salt
pinch of cream of tartar
cooking spray
parchment paper
1 ganache recipe

Place rack in the center of the oven and preheat oven to 375 degrees. Spray the insides of three soup cans with cooking spray. Place the cans on a piece of parchment paper and trace the circumference of each with a pencil. Cut out 3 rounds of parchment and line the bottom of each can with a paper round. Place cans on a baking sheet and set aside. In food processor, pulse chocolate into fine particles then place the chocolate in a small bowl and microwave on medium until the chocolate begins to melt, about 1 minute. Stir until smooth and let cool. Meanwhile, in same processor bowl, place walnuts and flour and pulse until walnuts are finely chopped about 10 to 15 seconds. In a medium mixing bowl, place the butter and sugar and beat until creamy. Add egg yolks, one at a time, beating well after each addition. Add vanilla with last yolk. Reduce mixer speed to low speed then beat in the melted chocolate. Using a wooden spatula, gently stir in the walnut mixture. Wash mixer beaters and dry them thoroughly. Place egg whites, salt, and cream of tartar in a small bowl and beat on high until the whites hold stiff peaks, about 60 to 90 seconds. Fold the egg white mixture thoroughly but gently into the chocolate mixture. Spoon the batter into the prepared cans, dividing it evenly. Bake the cakes until a toothpick inserted into the center of one comes out clean, about 30 minutes. Remove the cans from the oven and place them on a wire rack to cool. When the cakes have cooled, invert the cans over the wire rack to release them. Peel off the parchment paper and place the cakes upright on the racks. Pour about 3 tablespoons of lukewarm ganache over each cake, using a spatula to smooth the icing all over. Let the cakes stand until the ganache is firm, about 1 hour. The tortes will keep, covered, in the refrigerator for 2 to 3 days.

Ganache
1/4 cup plus 2 tablespoons heavy cream
5 ounces imported bittersweet chocolate, finely chopped

Pour cream into a small saucepan, bring to a boil. Remove from heat and add the chocolate. Let the mixture stand until the chocolate softens, about 1 minute, then stir with a whisk until the chocolate is melted. Allow ganache to cool slightly, then pour over cooled tortes.

Approximate servings per recipe: 3.
Per serving: Calories 823; Fat 60g;
Carbohydrates 64g; Fiber 6g; Protein 13g.

Food That Makes You Feel Good!

Heart's Desire Dessert Shots

4 Heart's Desire cookies
1 cup vanilla pudding
4 tablespoon whipped cream
4 teaspoons chocolate syrup
Sprinkles, optional
4 (2 ounce) shot glasses

Break cookies into quarters and press one-quarter cookie into the bottom of each glass. Top with a teaspoon of pudding then repeat the process, ending with a cookie. Top with a teaspoon of whipped topping, drizzle with chocolate syrup, dust with sprinkles, if using. Refrigerate at least 2 hours before serving.

Approximate servings per recipe: 4.
Per serving: Calories 210; Fat 8g; Carbohydrates 32g; Fiber 1g; Protein 4g.

A Heart's Desire Dessert Shot is perfectly sized so you can have your cake and eat it, too!

Heart's Desire Cookie

A flourless, butterless, yolkless cookie
3/4 cup of unsweetened Dutch-process cocoa powder
2 1/2 cups powdered sugar
1/8 teaspoon salt
1 tablespoon pure vanilla extract
4 large egg whites
2 cups walnuts, coarsely chopped
parchment paper

Preheat oven to 350 degrees. Whisk together cocoa, sugar, and salt in a large bowl. Combine vanilla and egg whites in a cup, and then slowly add to the cocoa mix. Beat batter for 2 minutes. Stir in chopped walnuts. Drop 1/4-cup mounds of batter about three inched apart onto a large baking sheet lined with parchment. Place baking sheet on the middle rack of oven, reduce oven temperature to 325 degrees, and bake until small cracks appear in tops of cookies, 15 to 17 minutes. Cool completely before peeling from paper. Increase oven to 350 degrees then bake the next batch the same way.

Approximate servings per recipe: 24.
Per serving: Calories 155; Fat 7g; Carbohydrates 22g; Fiber 1g; Protein 3g.

Special Desserts

Pamper with Cream Puffs!

140

Food That Makes You Feel Good!

We are blessed that someone took time out of their life and stretched her body - ruining her figure! - just so we could come into this world.

God knows none of us would be here if not for our mother, and for that we owe her a huge debt of gratitude!

We should all take time -while we can - to show our mothers just how much we appreciate all they have done for us and there is no better way to show Mom just how much she means than to present her with a decadent, delightful and delicious dessert that she would never take the time to make for herself.

Most women, at any age, cannot resist over-the-top desserts and nothing says "over-the-top" quite like a cream puff, also known as a profiterole.

According to Webster's encyclopedia, the word profiterole, also spelled prophitrole, profitrolle and profiterolle has existed in English since the 16th century, although the original meaning in both English and French is unclear.

Later, profiterole came to mean a kind of roll "baked under the ashes."

In a 17th-century French cookbook, a recipe for a potage de profiterole describes it as a soup of dried small breads simmered in almond broth and garnished with cockscombs and truffles. Today's meaning, as used here, appears to be 19th century.

Although they look quite delicate and difficult to create, the classic cream puff indulgence is actually quite easy to master, so long as you have a strong mixing arm or something to match it.

I say this because to me the hardest part of making cream puffs is the beating of the eggs - individually - into the hot butter mixture. You must work quickly to prevent the egg from scrambling.

A strong forearm and good whisk are all that's required to accomplish this, but if you're lacking in muscle simply call for some help in the kitchen. It's a great excuse for company!

Cream puffs really do make you feel pampered and they are small enough to endulge in - in moderation - without causing harm to a diet. Plus, its a nice way to show someone how much you care.
Bon Appétit!

Special Desserts

Classic Cream Puffs

CHOUX PASTRY
1 cup water
1/2 cup butter, unsalted
1/4 teaspoon salt
1 cup all purpose flour
4 large eggs

FILLING
1 1/2 cups cold whole milk
5 1/8 ounces instant vanilla pudding
3/4 teaspoon pure vanilla extract
2 cups whipping cream, whipped

CHOCOLATE GLAZE
6 tablespoons cocoa powder
1 1/2 teaspoons shortening
1 teaspoon corn syrup
1/4 teaspoon ground cinnamon

Classic Cream Puffs are always a delight to receive and a pleasure to bite into!

PASTRY: Preheat oven to 400 degrees. In a saucepan bring water, butter and salt to a boil. Add flour all at once and stir until it forms a ball. Remove from heat, let stand 5 minutes. Add eggs, one at a time, beating well after each addition and until the mixture is smooth and not shiny. Drop by 1/4 cups onto a greased baking sheet. Bake at 400 degrees for 30-35 minutes or until lightly golden brown. Remove to a wire rack and let cool.
FILLING: In a bowl beat the milk, pudding mix and vanilla on low speed for 2 minutes. Let stand for 5 minutes then fold in whipped cream. Fill cream puffs by placing cream in a piping bag and piping it into the center of the puffs.
GLAZE: in a heavy saucepan, combine all glaze ingredients and cook over low heat, stirring until mixture is smooth. Drizzle chocolate glaze over cream puffs and chill for at least one hour prior to serving. Keep leftovers refrigerated.

Approximate servings per recipe: 8. Per serving: Calories 545; Fat 41g; Carbohydrates 38g; Fiber 1g; Sugar 21g; Protein 8g.

Food That Makes You Feel Good!

Strawberries 'n' Chocolate Cream Puffs

CHOUX PASTRY
1 cup water
1/2 cup butter, unsalted
1/4 teaspoon salt
1 cup all-purpose flour
3 tablespoons cocoa powder
4 large eggs

FILLING
16 ounces cream cheese, softened
1 cup granulated sugar
2 cups whipping cream, whipped
3 cups coarsely chopped fresh strawberries
powdered sugar for dusting

PASTRY: Preheat oven to 400 degrees. In a heavy saucepan over medium heat, bring water, butter and salt to a boil. Add flour and cocoa all at once, stir until a smooth ball forms. Remove from the heat, let stand 5 minutes. Add eggs, one at a time, beating well after each addition. Beat until smooth and not shiny. Drop batter by heaping tablespoonfuls onto greased or parchment lined baking sheets. Bake at 400 degrees for 30-35 minutes or until set and brown. Remove to wire racks and immediately split puffs open, removing any soft dough from inside. (Soft dough may be eaten or discarded.) Cool puffs completely.

FILLING: In a medium mixing bowl, beat cream cheese and sugar until fluffy. Fold in whipped cream and strawberries then fill bottom halves of puffs with the cream mixture, replace tops, and dust with powdered sugar just prior to serving.

Approximate servings per recipe: 15 puffs. Per serving: Calories 382; Fat 30g; Carbohydrates 24g; Fiber 1g; Sugar 15g; Protein 6g.

Special Desserts

Coconut Cream Puffs

CREAM PUFF
2 3/4 ounces reg. vanilla pudding mix
2 cups milk
1/2 cup sweetened flaked coconut
8 ounces crushed pineapple, well-drained
1/4 teaspoon rum extract
1 cup water
6 tablespoons butter
1 teaspoon salt
1/2 teaspoon sugar
3/4 cup flour
4 large eggs
ICING
1 cup powdered sugar
1 tablespoon water
6 tablespoons sweetened coconut

Cook pudding as directed, using milk. Place in medium bowl; cover surface with plastic wrap and chill at least 4 hours. When cool, fold in coconut and well drained pineapple and rum extract. Keep chilled.

Preheat oven to 425 degrees. In a heavy, medium saucepan over medium-low heat, heat water, butter, salt and sugar until butter melts. Remove from heat, stir in flour all at once, beating with a wooden spoon until smooth. Return to heat. Stir constantly - approximately 12-15 minutes - until dough leaves sides of pan, forming a smooth mass (dough should look slightly dry), remove from heat.

Make well in center of dough, add 1 egg at a time, beating vigorously with wooden spoon until all liquid is absorbed and reformed into smooth mass before adding next egg. Measure 1/4 cup of dough, place in mound on a lightly buttered baking sheet. Repeat, making 6 mounds. Top each with 1 tablespoon of remaining dough. Bake until puffed and golden, 20-25 minutes. Remove from oven. With sharp knife, make a small slit in each puff where large bottom connects with smaller top. Bake 10 more additional minutes then allow to cool on racks. Cut tops of cream puffs off with a serrated knife. Remove any moist dough inside, then fill each puff with the pudding mixture. Place tops back on. In the bowl of electric mixer, combine powdered sugar and water, beating until smooth. Drizzle icing over tops of the puffs and sprinkle with the coconut.

Approximate servings per recipe: 6. Per serving: Calories 480; Fat 23g; Sodium 692mg; Carbohydrate 61g; Fiber 1g; Sugar 42g; Protein 9g.

Food That Makes You Feel Good!

Lemon Cream Puffs

CHOUX PASTRY
1 cup water
1/2 cup butter, unsalted
1 pinch salt
1 cup flour
1/2 teaspoon pure lemon extract
4 eggs

FILLING
3 1/2 ounces lemon instant pudding mix
1/2 teaspoon pure lemon extract
1 1/2 cups milk
1 cup whipped topping
1/4 teaspoon poppy seeds, optional
powdered sugar for dusting

PASTRY: For filling, whisk milk and pudding until it thickens. Set aside in refrigerator. For the pastry, preheat oven to 400 degrees, and in a saucepan combine butter, water and salt. Bring to a boil and keeping on flame, add all the flour, mixing thoroughly. Remove pan from heat and add lemon extract then eggs, one at a time, beating until it loses its gloss and becomes doughy again.
Repeat this with all eggs then spoon batter by tablespoon onto a cookie sheet. Bake at 400 degrees for 15 minutes then turn the heat down to 250 degrees and finish baking for 20 minutes or until golden brown.
Remove from cookie sheet to wire rack and split puffs in half, removing (and eating) any soft dough inside. Let puffs cool.
FILLING: In a medium bowl, combine whipped topping, lemon extract, pudding mix and poppy seeds, if using. Fill puffs and keep chilled until serving. Dust with powdered sugar, if desired, right before serving.

Approximate servings per recipe: 15 puffs. Per serving: Calories 154; Fat 9g; Carbohydrates 14g; Fiber 0.2g; Sugar 6g; Protein 3g.

Special Desserts

Food That Makes You Feel Good!

Being the youngest of seven children in a family of very humble means doesn't sound like a blessing, but at times it sure felt like one because it meant my mother had to help make ends meet by running a tiny bakery - a gem that afforded us the luxury of fresh, delicious baked goods throughout youth.

Mom was strict and had a policy that we weren't allowed to touch, let alone eat, anything but rejects. This meant we had to wait until Mom inspected all the baked goods, deeming which were worthy and which were rejected before we got our hot little hands on them.

I didn't mind because it gave me snippets of time to sit and soak in all the sweet, warm scents swirling around Mom. Oh yes, I remember it well!

Later on in my youth that same sweet, scintillating scent drew me into a Dunkin' Donuts, the place where a girlfriend's mother baked. Ann Bencur was a very kind woman who gave us girls the divine delight of eating freshly made French Crullers right out of the pan! It was the first time I had ever tasted a French Cruller and none have quite compared since. They were hot, puffy and filling the air with their sweet perfume of melted sugar blending with warm and exotic vanilla spices.

When the cruller was finally cool enough to eat, I could hear myself moaning, "Oh my!" between every single bite. That experience, which had a profound and lasting impact on my palate, taught me that all doughnuts – especially French Crullers – are not created alike.

I also learned, quite frankly, that a doughnut not freshly made is a doughnut not worth eating.

This penchant for fresh baked goods has served me well, that is until I moved from a big city to little rural town and found myself literally up a creek without a doughnut shop!

Never one to let distance get in the way of doughnut enchantment, I set out to discover a way to make my favorite doughnuts myself.

After much trial and many an error, in the end I was able to kill more than two birds with one doughnut hole. Not only is it possible to make doughnuts like the store brands, but you can also do it for a heck of a lot less money, and you can do it all in the comfort and convenience of your very own home, no matter where it is!

Here are some favorite ways to enjoy some most delicious doughnuts, including a really quick one so you can enjoy a fresh, hot, flavorful and delicious doughnut just about anytime!

Special Desserts

Homemade doughnuts offer you hand-selected ingredients, fabulous freshness, lower prices and the sweet scent of doughnuts, all in the comfort and convenience of your very own home. It doesn't get any better than that!

The Do's of Donuts!

DO use a fat that is solid at room temperature, such as vegetable shortening. Doughnuts fried in a fat that is liquid at room temperature like canola or any other liquid oil will make your doughnuts **VERY** greasy, resulting in excessive fat absorption and doughnuts that are not palatable.

DO use all-purpose flour. Bread flour or self-rising (unless called for) will make doughnuts tough and chewy.

DO use real butter when called for. Margarine, substitutes or spreads often contain high amounts of water and other compounds, which can have a less than desirable effect on your end result.
If you don't normally use butter, keep some on hand in the freezer for the rare times you need it.

DO use eggs when called for. Crullers depend on the egg to rise as lightly as they do. Using a substitute can lead to a disastrous result.

DO make only what will be consumed. Donuts have a very short shelf life and will begin to go stale in just a few short hours.

Food That Makes You Feel Good!

My Favorite French Crullers

PASTRY
1 teaspoon granulated sugar
1 cup boiling water
1/2 cup butter
1 cup sifted all purpose flour
4 large eggs
1/2 teaspoon pure vanilla extract
vegetable shortening for frying

GLAZE
2 cups powdered sugar
1/4 cup unsweetend cocoa powder
1/4 cup milk
dash of vanilla extract

PASTRY: In a 2-quart saucepan, bring sugar, water and butter to a boil. Using a whisk, add flour and beat vigorously over direct heat until mixture becomes very thick and leaves the sides of the pan. Remove from heat and whisk in eggs, one at a time, beating hard after each addition. Add vanilla and beat mixture until glaze disappears.
In a Dutch oven, heat 2 inches of vegetable shortening to 365 degrees.
Place dough into a pastry bag then squeeze out dough into circles on pieces of greased waxed paper. Carefully turn paper upside down over pot so cruller will drop into hot shortening. Don't crowd pan, cook only 4 at a time.
Turn crullers over as soon as they become lightly brown, about 30-40 seconds. Remove cruller and drain on brown paper bags.
GLAZE: In a small bowl, combine powdered sugar, cocoa, milk and dash of vanilla in a small bowl. Drizzle over cruller.

Approximate servings per recipe: 24. Per serving: Calories 56; Fat 5g; Sodium 50 mg; Carbohydrates 6g; Fiber 0.14g; Sugar 2g; Protein 2g.

Special Desserts

Krispy Kurellas

PASTRY

1 1/2 cups warm milk (105 degrees)
1/2 cup granulated sugar
1/4 cup warm water (105 degrees)
2 (1/4 ounce) packages instant yeast
1 teaspoon fine sea salt
2 large eggs
1/3 cup solid shortening
5 cups all purpose flour
vegetable shortening for frying

GARNISH

1/2 cup Powdered Sugar

In saucepan, scald milk, add sugar and let cool. In mixing bowl, combine milk with water and yeast. Allow yeast to dissolve then add salt, eggs, shortening and 2 cups of flour. Beat on low for 30 seconds then raise speed to medium for 2 minutes. Stir in remaining flour and mix until smooth. Cover and let rise until dough doubles in size, about 1 hour. Turn dough onto a floured surface and gently roll out to 1/2 inch thickness. Cut with floured doughnut cutter. Cover doughnuts and let rise until doubled, about 40 minutes. In a Dutch oven, Heat 2 inches of shortening to 365 degrees. Slide doughnuts into hot oil, cooking 50 seconds then flipping to other side. Cook another 60 seconds and remove. Sprinkle with powdered sugar.

Approximate servings per recipe: 48. Per serving: Calories 131; Fat 5g; Carbohydrates 16g; Fiber 0.46g; Sugar 8g; Protein 2g.

Food That Makes You Feel Good!

Doughnuts Done Quick!

PASTRY
1 can (10 count) refrigerated biscuits vegetable shortening for frying

GLAZE
2 cups powdered sugar
1/4 cup unsweetend cocoa powder
1 teaspoon pure vanilla extract
1/4 cup milk

PASTRY: In a Dutch oven, heat 1 inch of shortening to 365 degrees. Separate biscuits, then using your thumb, press a hole through the center of each, giving it the appearance of a doughnut. Drop biscuit in hot shortening until brown, about 45 seconds, then turn over and fry until brown on the other side. Remove to drain on a brown paper bag.
GLAZE: In a small bowl, make glaze by stirring together the powdered sugar, cocoa, vanilla and milk. Dip doughnut into glaze then serve.

Approximate servings per recipe: 10. Per serving: Calories 94; Fat 4g; Sodium 324 mg; Carbohydrate 13g; Fiber 0.4g; Sugars 3g; Protein 2g.

Variation: Try filling these gems with your favorite jelly or pudding. Simply place filling in a pastry tube, omit placing the hole in center of the doughnut, then fill doughnut after it has been cooked. It's that easy and oh, so worth it!

Special Desserts

Hunting for Mousse

When my eyes first met the words "Chocolate Mousse" on a menu, my obviously uneducated brain instantly imagined it to be something along the lines of a hollow piece of chocolate shaped into a moose. You know, like those chocolate Easter bunnies, which intrigued me enough to order it.

I cannot tell you how surprised I was when I wasn't served the hollow hunk of chocolate I was expecting. What arrived in its place was perhaps the most splendid and superior swirl of sinful sweetness that ever slinked across my naïve lips. I was instantly enamored!

Mousse, which is French for "froth" or "foam," is a rich, airy preparation that has the versatility to be served hot or cold, savory or sweet, and though appearing complex has only three keys to creating: base, binder, and lightener.

The base is the principal flavoring agent, such as chocolate in a chocolate mousse or salmon in a salmon mousse. The binder is usually gelatin but sometimes the base ingredient has enough body that a binder is not required, such as in a chocolate or a cheese mousse.

A mousse is lightened by an aerator such as beaten egg whites or whipped cream to produce an airy texture. This needs to be mixed in gently to prevent it from deflating.

Cold dessert mousses are best served in decorative glasses, garnished with fruit, sweet sauces or whipped cream.

Mousse, which is French for "froth" or "foam," is a rich, airy preparation that, though appearing complex has only three keys to creating: base, binder, and lightener.

Food That Makes You Feel Good!

Chocolate Mousse

1 teaspoon unflavored gelatin
1 tablespoon cold water
2 tablespoons boiling water
1/2 cup sugar
1/4 cup unsweetend cocoa powder
1/2 pint cold heavy cream, whipped
1 teaspoon pure vanilla extract

Sprinkle gelatin over cold water in small bowl, let stand 1 minute to soften. Add boiling water and stir until gelatin is completely dissolved and mixture is clear. Cool slightly. Stir together sugar and cocoa in medium bowl; add whipping cream and vanilla. Beat at medium speed, scraping bottom of bowl occasionally, until mixture is stiff; pour in gelatin mixture and beat until well blended. Spoon mixture into serving dishes and refrigerate about 30 minutes.

Approximate servings per recipe: 4 Per serving: Calories 332; Fat 22g; Carbohydrates 30g; Fiber 1g; Protein 3g.

Cranberry Mousse

1 cup cranberry juice cocktail
1 (3 ounce) package raspberry gelatin
1 (16 ounce) can jellied cranberry sauce
1 cup heavy cream, whipped

In a saucepan, heat cranberry juice cocktail to boiling. Remove from heat and stir in raspberry gelatin until dissolved. Stir in cranberry sauce. Chill until mixture is thickened. Fold in whipped cream and pour into individual dishes or a decorative serving bowl. Chill until firm.
Garnish with additional whipped cream, if desired.

Approximate servings per recipe: 6 Per serving: Calories 327; Fat 14g; Carbohydrates 50g; Fiber 1g; Protein 2g.

Don't be anxious! Follow directions and you will always be pleased with your results!

Contact the Author
Laura Kurella is available for positive and uplifting public appearances, workshops, cooking demonstrations, speaking engagements and book signings.

Laura may be contacted through her publisher or by visiting her websites:
http://www.laurakurella.com
http://www.fabulouscookbooks.com

Isaac Publishing, Inc.
http://www.isaacpublishing.com
admin@isaacpublishing.com